Vanished

Strange & Mysterious Disappearances

Ethan Hayes

FREE REIGN

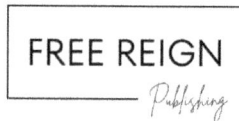

FREE REIGN

Publishing

Contents

Introduction

In the annals of human history, there are stories that defy explanation, events that challenge the boundaries of our understanding. Among these enigmas, few are as haunting and perplexing as the sudden and mysterious disappearances that leave behind only questions and shattered lives. These vanishings, often cloaked in an aura of the supernatural, push the limits of reality and force us to confront the possibility that our world is not as we perceive it.

In *Vanished: Strange and Mysterious Disappearances*, we delve into the shadowy realm where the ordinary meets the extraordinary. From isolated rural communities to bustling urban centers, the cases documented in this book span continents and centuries, yet they share a common thread of eerie inexplicability. What becomes of those who vanish without a trace? Are they victims of foul play, abducted by forces beyond our comprehension, or have they slipped into another dimension, lost to us forever?

Through meticulous research and chilling first-hand accounts, I invite you to journey into the unknown. Each chapter unravels a new mystery, presenting evidence and theories that range from the plausible to the fantastical. We will explore the haunted forests, desolate highways, and quiet towns where these disappearances occurred, seeking clues that may illuminate the dark secrets behind these unsettling events.

As with my previous works, *Fear in the Forest* and *What Lurks Beyond*, my aim was to entertain by presenting chilling true tales. This book is not merely a collection of unsolved mysteries but a testament to the enduring power of the unexplained. Whether you are a skeptic or a believer, the stories within these pages will challenge your perceptions and perhaps lead you to question the nature of reality itself.

Prepare to be intrigued, disturbed, and utterly captivated. The truth may be out there, but in the meantime, we have the stories—the inexplicable, the mysterious, the vanished.

Introduction

\- Ethan Hayes

2024

Chapter One

Amy Lynn Bradley

AMY LYNN BRADLEY, a 23-year-old from Virginia, vanished under mysterious circumstances during a

Caribbean cruise on the Royal Caribbean International's Rhapsody of the Seas in March 1998. Despite extensive searches and numerous alleged sightings, her case remains unsolved, leaving her family and investigators with more questions than answers.

On March 21, 1998, the Bradley family embarked on a week-long Caribbean cruise, departing from San Juan, Puerto Rico, with stops including Aruba and Curaçao. Amy, who had recently graduated from Longwood University and was about to start a new job, was initially reluctant to join the cruise but eventually decided to accompany her family.

The night before her disappearance, Amy and her brother Brad attended a dance party on the ship. They returned to their cabin around 3:30 a.m. on March 24, 1998, and chatted on the balcony until approximately 5:30 a.m. When Brad went to sleep, Amy mentioned she might get off the ship in Curaçao to buy cigarettes.

At around 6:00 a.m., Ron Bradley, Amy's father, woke up and found the balcony door slightly open, but Amy was nowhere to be found. The family searched the ship and alerted the crew, but the ship's staff did not make an announcement or prevent passengers from disembarking until several hours later, by which time many passengers had already left the ship.

The initial response from the cruise ship staff and

subsequent investigation raised numerous concerns. The Bradley family criticized the ship's crew for not immediately announcing Amy's disappearance or thoroughly searching all cabins, including those of staff and passengers. The ship docked in Curaçao as scheduled, giving any potential abductors an opportunity to take Amy ashore.

Witnesses reported seeing Amy in the early morning hours of March 24. Two passengers saw her taking an elevator to the ship's top deck around 6:00 a.m. Another witness claimed to have seen Amy with a member of the ship's band, known as "Yellow," near the dance club. This band member was seen returning alone a short time later.

In the years following her disappearance, there have been several alleged sightings of Amy. In August 1998, two Canadian tourists reported seeing a woman matching Amy's description on a beach in Curaçao. The woman had tattoos identical to Amy's: a Tasmanian Devil on her shoulder, a sun on her lower back, a Chinese symbol on her right ankle, and a lizard around her navel. Another potential sighting occurred in January 1999, when a U.S. Navy officer claimed to have met a woman in a brothel in Curaçao who identified herself as Amy Lynn Bradley and begged for help.

Numerous theories have emerged regarding Amy's

disappearance. Some believe she may have been abducted and sold into human trafficking. This theory is supported by various alleged sightings and the nature of her last known interactions on the ship. For instance, Amy's family noted that certain crew members had shown an unusual amount of interest in her, with one waiter even asking her to join him at a bar during a stop in Aruba, which she declined.

Another theory suggests that Amy may have fallen victim to foul play involving the ship's crew or passengers. The Bradleys hired private investigators and continued to push for answers, leading to various leads, but none conclusive.

In one disturbing incident, Amy's family was contacted by Frank Jones, who claimed to be a former U.S. Army Special Forces officer. He told them he had seen Amy being held by heavily armed men in a housing complex in Colombia and described her tattoos accurately. The Bradleys paid Jones over $200,000 to fund a rescue operation that never materialized. Jones was later convicted of defrauding the family and sentenced to prison.

The search for Amy involved multiple agencies, including the FBI and the Netherlands Antilles Coast Guard. Search dogs were used on the ship, and the surrounding waters were combed for evidence. Despite these efforts, no trace of Amy was found.

Over the years, the Bradleys have remained vigilant, keeping Amy's case in the public eye through media appearances and a dedicated website. The FBI continues to offer a reward for information leading to Amy's recovery and the prosecution of those responsible for her disappearance.

In 2005, a woman resembling Amy was reportedly seen in a department store in Barbados, accompanied by three men who threatened her. The witness described the woman as distraught and claiming to be from Virginia. Composite sketches were created based on this account, but no further information was obtained.

In 2010, a jawbone washed ashore in Aruba. Initially thought to be connected to another missing person's case, Natalee Holloway, it was later determined not to be hers. No further testing was done, leaving open the possibility that it could belong to one of several missing individuals, including Amy.

Theories about Amy's fate continue to circulate, ranging from abduction and trafficking to more sinister possibilities involving maritime crime. Despite extensive investigation and numerous tips, her disappearance remains one of the most perplexing and heartbreaking mysteries in recent history.

As the years pass, the search for Amy continues, driven by the determination to uncover the truth and bring closure to a family that has endured unimaginable anguish.

Chapter Two

Paula Jean Welden

THE DISAPPEARANCE of Paula Jean Welden on December 1, 1946, is one of the most enduring mysteries in Vermont's history. An 18-year-old sophomore at Bennington College, Paula vanished while hiking on the Long Trail, a 273-mile hiking route that extends through the forests and mountains of Vermont. Despite extensive searches and numerous theories, no trace of her has ever been found. Her case not only captivated the nation but also led to significant changes in the state's law enforcement infrastructure.

* * *

Paula Jean Welden was a typical college student in many respects. She was studying art at Bennington College, though she had expressed interest in switching her major to botany. She worked part-time in the college dining hall and was known to be an adventurous and outdoorsy young woman who enjoyed hiking, camping, and other outdoor activities.

On the afternoon of December 1, 1946, Paula told her roommate that she was going to take a break from studying and go for a hike on the Long Trail. She left Dewey Hall at approximately 2:30 PM, wearing a red parka, blue jeans, and white sneakers—not the most suitable attire for the cold weather. Paula had little money with her, having left behind an uncashed check from her parents.

Paula was last seen hitchhiking near the Bennington campus around 2:45 PM, where a motorist gave her a ride to the trailhead near Glastenbury Mountain.

Several witnesses saw her walking along the trail later that afternoon. One of the last people to see her was a man named Louis Knapp, who spoke with her around 4:00 PM. She asked him about the trail's length before continuing on her way.

The sun set around 5:00 PM, and shortly afterward, it began to snow. Paula did not return to her dormitory that evening, but her roommate assumed she was studying late. It was only the next morning, when she failed to attend her classes, that Paula was reported missing.

The search for Paula was immediate but disorganized, largely due to Vermont's lack of a state police force at the time. The college organized search parties composed of students and faculty, but their efforts were hampered by the snowy conditions and lack of proper equipment. As days passed with no sign of Paula, the search expanded to include firefighters, the National Guard, and even the Connecticut State Police.

Paula's father, Archibald Welden, was particularly critical of the local authorities' handling of the search. He enlisted the help of Governor Ernest Gibson, who called in additional support from neighboring states. Despite these efforts, no trace of Paula was ever found on or near the trail.

In the days following Paula's disappearance, several

eyewitnesses came forward with potential leads. A waitress in Fall River, Massachusetts, claimed to have seen a disturbed young woman matching Paula's description in a diner the day after she vanished, but this lead proved inconclusive. A train conductor reported seeing her in South Carolina, but this too led nowhere.

One of the more intriguing leads involved a man named Fred Gadette, a lumberjack who lived near the Long Trail. Gadette reportedly made several conflicting statements about his whereabouts on the day Paula disappeared and even claimed to know where she was buried. However, he later recanted these statements, claiming he was seeking attention. Despite being considered a person of interest, no evidence was found to link him to Paula's disappearance.

Over the years, numerous theories have emerged regarding Paula's fate. These range from the plausible to the fantastical:

1. Accidental Death: One of the most straightforward theories is that Paula got lost or injured on the trail and succumbed to the elements. The sudden snowfall and cold temperatures would have made survival difficult without proper gear.

2. Suicide: Some have speculated that Paula may have been depressed and chose to end her life in the

wilderness. However, those who knew her, including her family, refuted this theory, citing her generally positive outlook and future plans.

3. Foul Play: Given the lack of evidence, many believe Paula met with foul play. Suspects include local residents like Fred Gadette and others who might have encountered her on the trail. However, without any physical evidence, this theory remains speculative.

4. Voluntary Disappearance: Another theory is that Paula chose to disappear and start a new life else-where. Supporters of this theory point to the fact that she had been feeling stressed about her studies and future. Yet, those close to her found this highly unlikely.

5. The Bennington Triangle: Paula's disappearance is one of several mysterious vanishings in the Bennington area between 1945 and 1950. This cluster of disappearances has led some to speculate about supernatural or paranormal causes, dubbing the area the "Bennington Triangle".

The mishandling of Paula Jean Welden's case had significant repercussions. Her father and others pushed for the establishment of a professional state law enforcement agency, leading to the creation of the Vermont

State Police in 1947. This was one positive outcome from an otherwise tragic situation.

Paula's disappearance has remained a topic of interest and speculation for decades. It inspired several works of fiction, including Shirley Jackson's novel "Hangsaman" and Hillary Waugh's "Last Seen Wearing...".

* * *

The case of Paula Jean Welden is a haunting reminder of how easily a person can vanish without a trace. Despite extensive searches, numerous theories, and ongoing interest, Paula's fate remains a mystery. Her disappearance not only impacted her family and community but also led to significant changes in Vermont's approach to law enforcement and search and rescue operations. As the years go by, the hope for answers persists, keeping Paula Jean Welden's story alive in the annals of unsolved mysteries.

Chapter Three

Jodi Huisentruit

THE DISAPPEARANCE OF JODI HUISENTRUIT, a beloved news anchor from Mason City, Iowa, has puzzled investigators and captivated the public for nearly three decades. On June 27, 1995, Jodi vanished without a trace, leaving behind a mystery that has yet to be solved. This chapter delves into the detailed accounts of her disappearance, the investigation, and the various theories that have emerged over the years.

* * *

Jodi Sue Huisentruit was born on June 5, 1968, in Long Prairie, Minnesota. She was a vibrant and ambitious woman who pursued a career in journalism, eventually becoming the morning news anchor for KIMT-TV in Mason City, Iowa. Known for her cheerful demeanor and professionalism, Jodi quickly became a well-liked figure in the community.

On the morning of June 27, 1995, Jodi was scheduled to report to work at 3:00 AM. When she failed to arrive, her colleague, Amy Kuns, called her at home around 4:00 AM. Jodi answered the phone, stating that she had overslept and would be at the station shortly. This was the last time anyone heard from her.

When Jodi did not show up by 7:00 AM, her colleagues grew concerned and contacted the police. Officers arrived at her apartment complex, Key Apartments, and found her red Mazda Miata in the parking lot. The scene around her car indicated a struggle: a pair of red dress shoes, a blow dryer, a bottle of hair spray, earrings, and her car keys were scattered on the ground.

Neighbors reported hearing a scream around 4:30 AM, and one witness saw a white or light-colored van in the parking lot at the same time. Despite these clues, the investigation struggled to find concrete leads.

Inside Jodi's apartment, police found no signs of forced entry or struggle. However, the raised toilet seat led some to speculate that she might have had a male guest, though this theory was never confirmed. Early in the investigation, John Vansice, a friend of Jodi's, came forward. Vansice, who was 22 years older than Jodi, claimed that she had visited his apartment the night before to watch a videotape of her recent surprise birthday party. Despite being cooperative and passing a polygraph test, Vansice remained a person of interest for many years.

* * *

Ongoing Investigation and Theories

- Stalker Theory: In the months leading up to her disappearance, Jodi had expressed concerns about being stalked. She reported to the Mason City Police that a man in a white truck had been following her. Despite this report, the stalker was never identified.

Some believe that this unknown individual could have been responsible for her abduction.

- John Vansice: Vansice's close relationship with Jodi and his proximity to her in the days before her disappearance made him a key figure in the investigation. In 2017, authorities obtained a search warrant for GPS data from his vehicles, but no incriminating evidence was found. Vansice has consistently maintained his innocence and denied any romantic involvement with Jodi.
- Other Theories: Various other theories have been proposed, including the possibility of a random abduction by an unknown assailant. Over the years, numerous leads and tips have surfaced, but none have led to a definitive breakthrough.

Despite extensive searches and numerous interviews, Jodi Huisentruit's case remains unsolved. Her disappearance has inspired multiple media productions, including episodes of "20/20" and "Unsolved Mysteries," as well as a dedicated podcast, "FindJodi."

In 2008, an anonymous individual sent copies of

Jodi's personal journal to a local newspaper. The sender was later identified as the wife of a former Mason City police chief, though the motive for sending the journal remains unclear.

Efforts to keep Jodi's memory alive continue. In 2015, the Iowa House of Representatives proposed declaring June 27 as Jodi Huisentruit Day, but the motion was ultimately declined. Private investigators, like Steve Ridge, and Jodi's family persist in their search for answers. In 2023, a $50,000 reward was offered for information leading to the recovery of her remains.

Jodi Huisentruit's disappearance is a haunting case that exemplifies the challenges of missing person investigations. Despite the passage of time, the hope for closure remains strong among those who knew and loved her. The continued efforts to solve her case are a testament to her impact on the community and the enduring quest for justice.

The investigation into Jodi Huisentruit's disappearance remains active, with law enforcement and private investigators still pursuing leads. As new technologies and methods of investigation develop, there is hope that one day the mystery of what happened to Jodi will be solved, bringing peace to her family and friends.

Chapter Four

Emanuela Orlandi

THE DISAPPEARANCE OF EMANUELA ORLANDI, a 15-year-old Vatican citizen, remains one of Italy's most enduring mysteries. On June 22, 1983, Emanuela vanished after leaving her music lesson in Rome, and despite decades of investigation, her fate is still unknown.

* * *

Emanuela Orlandi was the daughter of Ercole Orlandi, a Vatican employee, and lived with her family within Vatican City. On the day of her disappearance, Emanuela left home to attend a music lesson at the Tommaso Ludovico Da Victoria School. She spoke to her sister over the phone around 5:00 PM, mentioning that a man had approached her with a job offer to distribute Avon products. She was last seen at a bus stop, waiting to return home.

The initial response to Emanuela's disappearance involved routine checks, but as hours turned into days, the investigation intensified. The Vatican police, Italian law enforcement, and Interpol were all involved. Pope John Paul II made a public appeal for Emanuela's safe return, signaling the seriousness of the case.

The investigation received numerous tips and leads, many of which turned out to be false. A series of mysterious phone calls began to emerge, each providing conflicting information about Emanuela's whereabouts. One of the first significant leads came from a man who identified himself as "Pierluigi." He claimed his girlfriend had seen Emanuela in Campo dei Fiori, playing the flute and selling cosmetics. Another caller, "Mario," reported seeing her with two girls near Ponte Vittorio. These leads, however, led nowhere definitive.

Eyewitness accounts were numerous but inconsistent. Some claimed to have seen Emanuela in various parts of Rome, while others reported sightings in different countries. One particularly chilling account came from a man with an American accent, who claimed to represent a terrorist organization. He demanded the release of Mehmet Ali Ağca, the Turkish man who attempted to assassinate Pope John Paul II in 1981, in exchange for Emanuela's freedom. This caller, referred to as "the American," provided details such as Emanuela's music school ID and a receipt, lending some credibility to his claims.

Over the years, several theories have been proposed to explain Emanuela's disappearance. Here are some of the most prominent:

1. Terrorist Plot: One of the earliest theories suggested that Emanuela was kidnapped by a terrorist group seeking to leverage her release for Ağca's freedom. This theory gained traction due to the calls from "the American" and the apparent knowledge the callers had about Emanuela's possessions.

2. Criminal Organizations: Another theory

involves the Banda della Magliana, a notorious Roman criminal organization. In 2005, an anonymous tip led investigators to the tomb of Enrico De Pedis, a gang leader. While no concrete evidence was found in his tomb, his girlfriend claimed De Pedis had confessed to kidnapping Emanuela, suggesting a link between the mafia and her disappearance.

3. Vatican Conspiracy: Perhaps the most disturbing theory involves the Vatican itself. Some believe that high-ranking officials were involved in a cover-up, possibly linked to financial scandals or even sexual exploitation. Father Gabriele Amorth, the Vatican's chief exorcist, claimed that Emanuela had been kidnapped for sex parties organized by a member of the Vatican police. According to Amorth, Emanuela was later murdered, and her body disposed of in secret.

4. Human Trafficking: Another theory posits that Emanuela was abducted by human traffickers. This is supported by several reported sightings of her in various locations, including a claim that she was seen in a Middle Eastern brothel years after her disappearance. However, none of these sightings have been verified.

5. Mistaken Identity: Some suggest that Emanuela might have been mistaken for another

target or that her disappearance was a result of a personal vendetta. This theory is less supported by evidence but remains a possibility given the lack of concrete leads.

In recent years, renewed efforts have been made to solve the mystery. In 2018, construction workers found human bones near the Vatican embassy, sparking speculation that they might belong to Emanuela. However, forensic tests revealed the bones were too old to be hers. In 2019, the Orlandi family received an anonymous tip suggesting Emanuela's remains were in the Teutonic Cemetery within the Vatican. Two tombs were opened, but they contained no evidence related to Emanuela.

In 2023, Vatican prosecutors reopened the case, prompted by new information and public pressure. The Orlandi family continues to search for answers, hoping for closure after decades of uncertainty.

* * *

The disappearance of Emanuela Orlandi remains one of the most baffling and tragic mysteries of modern times. Despite extensive investigations, numerous theories, and countless tips, her fate is still unknown. The case highlights the complexities and challenges of solving disappearances, especially when they involve powerful institutions and potential conspiracies. As new leads continue to emerge, the hope remains that one day, the truth about Emanuela Orlandi will finally be uncovered, bringing peace to her family and shedding light on one of the Vatican's darkest mysteries.

Chapter Five

Frederick Valentich

THE MYSTERIOUS DISAPPEARANCE of Frederick Valentich remains one of aviation's most perplexing cases. On October 21, 1978, the 20-year-old Australian pilot vanished while flying a Cessna 182L over the Bass Strait. Valentich's last communication with air traffic control described a strange aircraft with unusual lights that seemed to be toying with him before he and his plane disappeared without a trace.

* * *

Frederick Valentich departed from Moorabbin Airport near Melbourne for a routine training flight to King Island, located 125 miles across the Bass Strait. He was an enthusiastic but relatively inexperienced pilot with about 150 hours of flying time. Valentich planned to make the round trip to pick up some friends and return the same evening.

At 7:06 PM, Valentich radioed Melbourne Flight Service to report an unidentified aircraft following him at 4,500 feet. He described the object as having four bright landing lights and a shiny, metallic exterior. Valentich stated that the aircraft passed over him at high speed and was orbiting above his plane. Over the next several minutes, Valentich's descriptions grew more alarming. He reported that the aircraft was not a conventional airplane and mentioned experiencing engine problems.

His final transmission was chilling: "It isn't an aircraft," Valentich said before the radio cut off with a metallic scraping sound. This was the last anyone heard from him. An immediate search was launched but failed to find any trace of Valentich or his aircraft.

The initial search for Valentich involved both sea and air efforts across the Bass Strait. Despite extensive operations, no wreckage or physical evidence of the plane was found. The Australian Department of Transport conducted an investigation but could not determine the cause of the disappearance. The case was officially closed with Valentich presumed dead, but the mystery was far from resolved.

In 1983, five years after the disappearance, an engine cowl flap from a Cessna 182L was discovered on Flinders Island. The Bureau of Air Safety Investigation confirmed that the part was from the same type of aircraft Valentich had flown, with serial numbers in the same range as his plane. However, this discovery did not provide any conclusive evidence regarding what happened to Valentich.

Several eyewitnesses came forward with reports that added layers of intrigue to the case. Some individuals claimed to have seen strange lights or aircraft in the area around the time of Valentich's disappearance. These accounts fueled speculation about the involvement of unidentified flying objects (UFOs). A group of ufologists from Phoenix, Arizona, known as Ground Saucer Watch, analyzed photos taken near the scene, which they claimed showed a fast-moving object exiting the water. Although the images were too blurry to provide definitive proof, they contributed to the growing UFO theory.

Another theory suggested that Valentich might have become disoriented while flying at night and experienced a phenomenon known as "graveyard spiral." This occurs when a pilot, believing they are maintaining a level flight, actually spirals downwards due to a loss of visual reference. This theory posits that the bright lights Valentich reported could have been celestial objects such as Venus, Mars, Mercury, and the star Antares, which he might have misidentified due to his disorientation.

The most sensational theory regarding Valentich's disappearance involves an encounter with a UFO. Valentich's own descriptions of the unidentified aircraft and its behavior suggested something out of the ordinary. He mentioned a green light and a metallic exterior, and his belief that the aircraft was playing a game with him before it seemingly caused his engine trouble. Ufologists argue that Valentich was either abducted by aliens or his aircraft was destroyed by a UFO. This theory is bolstered by the fact that Valentich was reportedly an ardent believer in UFOs and had expressed concerns about encountering one.

Eyewitnesses also claimed to have seen green lights in the sky near the Bass Strait around the time of Valentich's disappearance. Despite these reports, no concrete evidence has ever been found to support the UFO hypothesis. Nonetheless, it remains a popular explanation among conspiracy theorists and UFO enthusiasts.

Frederick Valentich's personal and psychological state at the time of his disappearance has also been scrutinized. Valentich had a strong interest in becoming a commercial pilot but had been rejected by the Royal Australian Air Force twice due to inadequate educational qualifications. He had also failed his commercial pilot's examinations on multiple occasions and had received several warnings for flying into restricted airspace and clouds. These setbacks may have affected his mental state and decision-making abilities during the flight.

Some theorists suggest that Valentich might have staged his own disappearance, although this idea lacks substantial evidence. The absence of a body or wreckage, combined with his final transmission, makes this theory less plausible. Additionally, there were no indications that Valentich had planned to disappear voluntarily.

* * *

The disappearance of Frederick Valentich remains one of aviation's most enduring mysteries. Despite extensive searches, investigations, and numerous theories, the exact circumstances of his vanishing have never been determined. Whether it was a tragic accident, a case of disorientation, or an encounter with the unknown, Valentich's last flight continues to fascinate and puzzle investigators, ufologists, and the public alike.

Until more evidence emerges, Frederick Valentich's disappearance will remain a topic of speculation and intrigue, a mysterious chapter in the annals of unsolved disappearances.

Chapter Six

Lynne Schulze

THE MYSTERIOUS DISAPPEARANCE of Lynne Schulze has puzzled investigators and her family for over five decades. An 18-year-old freshman at Middlebury College, Lynne vanished on December 10, 1971, in Middlebury, Vermont. Despite extensive searches and numerous theories, her case remains unsolved.

* * *

Lynne Kathryn Schulze was an adventurous and outgoing student from Simsbury, Connecticut. She enrolled at Middlebury College in the fall of 1971, eager to embrace her new life in Vermont. Described as a diligent student, Lynne kept journals and wrote weekly letters to her family, reflecting her close ties with them. Although she experienced homesickness and had considered withdrawing from school, she registered for the spring semester, indicating her intention to continue her education.

On December 10, 1971, Lynne was preparing for her final exams before the Christmas break. That morning, she spent time with friends studying for her English drama exam, scheduled for 1:00 PM. Around 12:55 PM, Lynne left her dormitory, telling her friends she needed to retrieve a favorite pen from her room. She never returned.

Eyewitnesses last saw Lynne at 2:15 PM standing on Court Street, near a bus stop and a health food store called All Good Things. She left behind all her personal belongings, including her identification and checkbook, suggesting she did not plan to be gone long.

The initial response to Lynne's disappearance was sluggish. Campus security was notified two days after she was last seen, but her parents were not informed until a week later. By then, any potential leads had grown cold. Extensive searches of the college campus, the surrounding areas, and local businesses yielded no significant clues.

Over the years, several theories and leads have emerged. One significant development came in 2015, when authorities began investigating Robert Durst, a real estate millionaire with a history of involvement in suspicious disappearances. Durst and his wife owned All Good Things, the health food store near where Lynne was last seen.

Robert Durst became a person of interest due to his proximity to the store where Lynne was last seen buying dried prunes around 12:30 PM on the day of her disappearance. Durst's connection to other missing persons and his criminal history, including the suspected murder of his wife Kathleen Durst and the confirmed killing of Morris Black, cast further suspicion on him. However, no physical evidence directly linking Durst to Lynne's disappearance has been found.

Multiple eyewitness accounts and theories have surfaced over the years:

1. Eyewitness Sightings: Some reports suggested

Lynne was seen hitchhiking southbound on Route 7, but these sightings were never confirmed.

2. Voluntary Disappearance: Lynne had mentioned the idea of faking her own death and starting anew. However, her family and friends doubted she would follow through with such a plan, especially considering she had registered for the spring semester and left all her personal items behind.

3. Foul Play: Given the circumstances and her sudden disappearance, foul play has always been a strong possibility. The involvement of Robert Durst added weight to this theory, but definitive evidence remains elusive.

Over the years, several individuals have falsely confessed to involvement in Lynne's disappearance. These confessions were investigated but ultimately dismissed as they provided no credible evidence or led to dead ends. The lack of concrete evidence has made it challenging to validate any single theory conclusively.

Lynne's disappearance profoundly affected her family. Her parents passed away in the 1990s without knowing what happened to their daughter. Her sister continues to seek answers and hopes for a resolution to the case. The emotional toll on the family is a poignant reminder of the enduring pain caused by such unresolved mysteries.

The disappearance of Lynne Schulze remains one of Vermont's most enduring unsolved mysteries. Despite numerous investigations, leads, and theories, her fate is still unknown. The involvement of Robert Durst added a layer of intrigue but also highlighted the complexities and challenges in solving long-standing missing persons cases. As of now, the search for answers continues, driven by the hope that one day, the mystery of Lynne Schulze's disappearance will be resolved.

If you have any information regarding the disappearance of Lynne Schulze, please contact the Middlebury Police Department at 802-388-3191.

Chapter Seven

Zebb Quinn

ON THE EVENING of January 2, 2000, Zebb Quinn finished his shift at Walmart and met his coworker, Robert Jason Owens, to look at a Mitsubishi Eclipse that Owens had told him about. The two were captured on surveillance cameras at the Eblen Citgo gas station purchasing sodas around 9:15 PM. Shortly thereafter, they left the station in separate vehicles, heading toward Long Shoals Road.

According to Owens, while they were driving, Quinn flashed his headlights, signaling Owens to pull over. Quinn told Owens he had received a page and needed to return a call. After making the call from a nearby payphone, Quinn appeared frantic and abruptly canceled their plans, stating he needed to leave. Owens claimed Quinn then rear-ended his truck before driving off. This would be the last confirmed sighting of Quinn.

Two weeks after Quinn's disappearance, on January 16, 2000, his car was found abandoned in the parking lot of the Little Pigs Barbecue restaurant, close to Mission St. Joseph's Hospital, where Quinn's mother and grandmother worked. The car presented several strange clues: the headlights were on, a large pair of lips and an exclamation mark were drawn in lipstick on the rear windshield, and inside was a live black Labrador-mix puppy that did not belong to Quinn. Additionally, the car contained several drink bottles, a jacket not belonging to Quinn, and a plastic hotel key card that could not be traced to any hotel.

Owens immediately became a person of interest due to his contradictory statements and peculiar actions. On January 4, two days after Quinn vanished, someone called Walmart claiming to be Quinn and reported that he was sick. The call was traced back to a Volvo plant where Owens worked. Owens admitted to making the call but insisted it was at Quinn's request.

Owens also claimed to have been involved in a separate car accident the night Quinn disappeared, which he said occurred near a Waffle House. However, no accident report was filed, and the injuries he sustained were inconsistent with a vehicular collision. His erratic behavior and the inconsistencies in his story made him the prime suspect.

One of the most puzzling aspects of the case was the page Quinn received on the night he disappeared. Investigators traced the call to the home of Quinn's aunt, Ina Ustich. However, Ustich denied making the call, stating she was having dinner with her friend Tamra Taylor at the time. Tamra Taylor is the mother of Misty Taylor, with whom Quinn had a potential romantic involvement, and Misty's boyfriend, Wesley Smith, was also present at the dinner. This discovery added another layer of complexity, as both Taylor and Smith were considered as potential suspects.

For years, the case went cold with little progress. Then, in March 2015, Owens was arrested for the murders of Cristie Schoen Codd, her husband Joseph Codd, and their unborn child. The investigation into these murders led to a search of Owens's property, where authorities found "fabric, leather materials, and unknown hard fragments" under a layer of concrete. These findings reignited interest in Quinn's case.

In 2017, Owens was indicted for first-degree murder in connection with Quinn's disappearance. During his plea deal in 2022, Owens accused his uncle, Gene Owens, of murdering Quinn. He claimed that Gene, hired by Wesley Smith, had lured Quinn and him to the Pisgah National Forest under the pretense of meeting Misty Taylor and subsequently killed Quinn. Owens claimed to have witnessed the murder and helped in disposing of Quinn's body, which was allegedly dismembered and burned.

Several theories have emerged over the years about what happened to Zebb Quinn:

1. Abduction and Murder by Acquaintances: The most supported theory involves Quinn being murdered by people he knew, possibly due to his involvement with Misty Taylor. This theory gained traction after Owens's partial confession and the discovery of incriminating evidence on his property.

2. Voluntary Disappearance: Some have speculated that Quinn may have disappeared voluntarily due to stress or personal issues. However, this theory

is widely dismissed by his family and friends, who describe Quinn as responsible and close to his loved ones.

3. Mistaken Identity or Random Crime: Another theory is that Quinn may have been the victim of a random crime or mistaken identity. However, the specific and personal nature of the clues found, such as the lipstick marks and the page from his aunt's home, make this theory less likely.

The disappearance of Zebb Quinn remains one of North Carolina's most haunting mysteries. Despite the partial resolution provided by Owens's confessions and subsequent guilty plea, many questions remain unanswered. The involvement of multiple parties, the strange behavior of Owens, and the enigmatic clues left behind continue to perplex investigators and haunt those who knew Zebb Quinn. As new information occasionally comes to light, the hope persists that one day the full truth of what happened to Zebb Quinn will be uncovered, providing closure to his family and friends.

Chapter Eight

Natasha Ryan

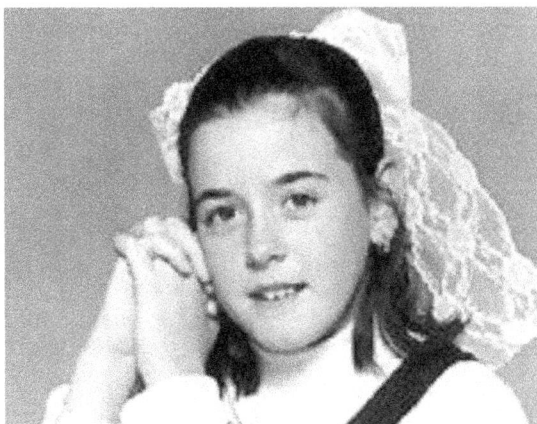

NATASHA RYAN, known as "the girl in the cupboard," became the center of one of Australia's most perplexing missing person cases when she vanished in 1998 at the age of 14. Her disappearance, presumed death, and subsequent discovery alive five years later, hiding just kilometers from her home, captured the nation's attention and sparked widespread media frenzy.

* * *

Natasha Ryan, a teenager from Rockhampton, Queensland, had a history of running away from home. In July 1998, she disappeared while walking the family dog. She was found days later at an outdoor music venue and had been staying with her boyfriend, Scott Black. Black was charged with abduction, but the charge was later dropped, and he was fined for obstructing the investigation.

On August 31, 1998, Natasha's mother dropped her off at North Rockhampton State High School. At some point during the day, Natasha disappeared again. Given her past behavior, the police initially believed she would return soon. However, as weeks turned into months, and other women in the area went missing, the assumption that Natasha was another runaway faded, giving rise to fears that she might have been the victim of a local serial killer.

The police launched an extensive search for Natasha, enlisting the help of over 100 local State Emergency Service volunteers. Witnesses reported seeing Natasha talking to an older man outside a cinema shortly before her disappearance, supporting the belief that she had run away. Despite this, the lack of contact and growing number of local disappearances suggested something more sinister.

Around the same time, Leonard Fraser, a convicted rapist, was implicated in the murders of several women in Rockhampton, including Beverly Leggo, Sylvia Benedetti, and Julie Turner. Fraser eventually confessed to killing Natasha, claiming he had met her at a movie theater, attacked her, and disposed of her body in a pond. Despite leading police to the remains of other victims, no evidence of Natasha's body was found, but the police accepted his confession, and Natasha's family held a memorial service for her on her 17th birthday.

Unbeknownst to her family and the authorities, Natasha was alive and living with Scott Black. For nearly five years, she resided in various homes around Rockhampton and the nearby coastal town of Yeppoon. Scott worked as a milkman and managed to keep Natasha hidden, even from close neighbors. She only went outside a handful of times, always under the cover of darkness, and spent most of her days indoors with the curtains drawn.

Contrary to popular belief, Natasha did not spend all her time in a cupboard. She would hide there only when visitors came. Otherwise, she moved freely around the house, engaging in activities like cooking, reading, sewing, and surfing the internet. The secrecy was so intense that Natasha made sanitary towels from bath towels to avoid Scott having to buy them and raising suspicion.

As Fraser's trial for Natasha's murder approached, guilt and fear may have weighed on her mind. In early April 2003, Natasha, using the name "Sally," contacted a children's counseling service and anonymously revealed her situation. This tip led the police to raid a house on Mills Avenue, where they found Natasha hiding in a bedroom cupboard.

Her discovery shocked everyone, especially since her family had long believed her to be dead. The prosecutor at Fraser's trial informed Natasha's father, who initially thought the police had found her body. It was a bitter-sweet moment when he realized she was alive.

The revelation of Natasha's whereabouts led to significant legal and social consequences. Scott Black was sentenced to one year in prison for perjury after falsely claiming he didn't know Natasha's location. Natasha was fined $4,000 and ordered to pay $16,000 towards the investigation costs for her role in the false police investigation.

Natasha and Scott later married in 2008 in a highly publicized and financially lucrative event. They secured media deals worth hundreds of thousands of dollars for exclusive rights to their story and wedding coverage. This profiting from the ordeal stirred public outrage, given the extensive resources and emotional toll invested in searching for Natasha.

Despite the public and media frenzy, Natasha's family struggled with her reappearance. Her mother, Jenny Ryan, expressed deep hurt and anger over the years of grief she had endured. Natasha herself acknowledged the pain she caused, but also stated that the reasons behind her disappearance might not fully justify her actions to her family.

Several theories emerged about why Natasha ran away and stayed hidden for so long. Some speculated that her troubled teenage years and desire to be with Scott, who was significantly older, motivated her actions. Others believed that Natasha felt trapped by the lies she had spun and saw no way to return without severe repercussions.

Natasha's case highlights the complexities of human behavior and the sometimes irrational decisions made under emotional distress. It also underscores the need for better mental health support for teenagers and the importance of understanding the deeper issues that lead to such drastic actions.

Natasha Ryan's disappearance and eventual reappearance remains a poignant and controversial chapter in Australian criminal history. Her story, filled with deception, emotional turmoil, and public spectacle, continues to be a subject of fascination and debate. As of today, Natasha, now known as Tash Black, lives a relatively private life with her husband and children, having moved past the shadow of her teenage years.

Chapter Nine

Ben McDaniel

On August 18, 2010, Ben McDaniel, a 30-year-old scuba diving enthusiast, vanished without a trace while exploring an underwater cave at Vortex Spring in Ponce de Leon, Florida. Despite extensive search efforts, no definitive evidence of his fate has been uncovered. .

* * *

Ben McDaniel was born on April 15, 1980, in Memphis, Tennessee. He was an experienced diver, having earned his open water diving certification at 14. Despite his enthusiasm, Ben faced significant personal challenges. His marriage had recently ended in divorce, and his construction business had failed, leaving him with a substantial debt of about $50,000 to the IRS. To help him cope, Ben's parents offered him their beach house in Santa Rosa Beach, Florida, where he moved to start afresh.

During his time in Florida, Ben frequently visited Vortex Spring, a popular diving location known for its underwater cave system. He became a familiar face at the dive shop and formed casual relationships with other divers and employees.

On August 18, 2010, Ben arrived at Vortex Spring. He completed a dive in the afternoon, during which he was observed studying the cave entrance carefully. After resurfacing, he filled his tanks, recorded in the dive shop's logs, and spent the remainder of the afternoon preparing for another dive.

Around 7:30 PM, as the sun began to set, Ben embarked on his final dive. Witnesses, including dive shop employees Chuck Cronin and Eduardo Taran, saw him enter the water and proceed towards the cave. Taran, aware that Ben had been known to force open the gate to the cave, unlocked it for him, watching as Ben descended into the depths. This would be the last confirmed sighting of Ben.

Ben's truck was discovered in the Vortex Spring parking lot the following morning, with his wallet, phone, and other personal belongings inside. His decompression tanks were found near the cave entrance, unused. When Ben failed to resurface, the Holmes County Sheriff's Office was contacted, and a search was initiated.

Experienced cave divers, including Edd Sorenson, conducted multiple dives into the cave system to locate Ben. Despite their efforts, no trace of Ben was found. Sorenson, who had explored the cave extensively, concluded that Ben was not in the cave, either dead or alive.

Several theories have emerged regarding Ben's disappearance:

1. Accidental Drowning: The most straightforward theory is that Ben drowned somewhere within the cave. However, extensive searches by experienced divers failed to locate his body or any equipment, which casts doubt on this explanation.

2. Foul Play: Some speculate that Ben was the victim of foul play. There are suggestions that he may have been murdered and his body removed from the area. However, there is no concrete evidence to support this theory.

3. Staged Disappearance: Another theory is that Ben staged his own disappearance to escape his financial and personal troubles. Supporters of this theory point to the fact that no trace of him was ever found, and the possibility that he might have used the dive as a cover to start a new life elsewhere.

4. Natural Causes: It's also possible that Ben encountered a natural hazard within the cave that caused his demise. This theory includes the possibility of his body being swept away by underwater currents or becoming trapped in an unsearched part of the cave.

Ben's family has been relentless in their search for answers. They hired private investigators and increased the reward for information leading to the discovery of Ben's body. Despite these efforts, no new evidence has emerged. The family even arranged for the issuance of a death certificate in 2013, although they continue to hope for closure.

Ben's case has drawn significant media attention,

featuring in documentaries like "Ben's Vortex" and episodes of "Disappeared." His disappearance has also sparked discussions about the safety and regulations of cave diving, highlighting the inherent dangers of the sport.

The disappearance of Ben McDaniel remains an unsolved mystery that haunts both the diving community and those who knew him. Whether he met with an accident, foul play, or chose to disappear voluntarily, the lack of definitive evidence leaves all possibilities open.

The quest for answers continues, driven by the hope and determination of Ben's family and the diving community. Until new evidence comes to light, the fate of Ben McDaniel remains open.

Chapter Ten

Brandon Lawson

ON THE NIGHT of August 8, 2013, Brandon Lawson, a 26-year-old father of four from San Angelo, Texas, disappeared under mysterious and alarming circumstances. His vanishing act, punctuated by a frantic 911 call, has baffled investigators, captivated true crime enthusiasts, and devastated his family.

* * *

Brandon Lawson lived with his longtime girlfriend, Ladessa Lofton, and their children. On the evening of his disappearance, Brandon and Ladessa had an argument, reportedly about his recent relapse into drug use and the stress of their long working hours. After the fight, Brandon left home, intending to drive to his father's house in Crowley, Texas, more than three hours away.

Around 11:30 PM, Brandon called his father to let him know he was on his way. At 12:30 AM on August 9, Brandon's truck ran out of gas on U.S. Route 277, near Bronte, Texas. He called his brother, Kyle Lawson, to ask for help, sounding panicked and claiming that "three Mexicans in the neighborhood" were chasing him. Kyle, suspecting Brandon might be hallucinating, reassured him and set out with his wife and child to bring a gas can to Brandon's location.

At 12:50 AM, Brandon made a chilling 911 call, which later became a focal point of the investigation. In the call, Brandon can be heard saying he needed the police and mentioning something about being "in the middle of a field," "pulled some guys over," and "one car here, the guy's chasing me into the woods". The call was difficult to understand due to poor reception and Brandon's apparent distress, but it clearly indicated he was in danger.

A trucker passing by reported Brandon's truck to the police at 12:56 AM, noting it was parked hazardously on the road. A Coke County deputy arrived around 1:00 AM, just as Kyle reached the scene with the gas can. Brandon, who had been on the phone with Kyle, claimed he could see him arriving but was nowhere to be found when Kyle and the deputy looked around.

Kyle initially thought Brandon might be hiding due to an outstanding warrant for his arrest on drug charges. He and the deputy inspected the area but found no sign of Brandon. Kyle waited in his car down the road for about 30 to 45 minutes, hoping Brandon would emerge once the deputy left, but he never did. By dawn, when Kyle returned to the truck, Brandon was still missing.

Authorities launched a comprehensive search involving thermal imaging cameras, aerial searches, and cadaver dogs. Despite these efforts, no trace of Brandon was found. Friends and family set up a Facebook page, "Help Find Brandon Lawson," to coordinate search efforts and gather tips.

Several theories emerged about what might have happened to Brandon:

1. Foul Play: Some believed Brandon's claims of being chased suggested he encountered foul play. The rugged terrain and presence of wildlife raised concerns that he might have been injured or worse.

2. Drug-Related Incident: Given Brandon's recent drug relapse and the paranoia evident in his calls, there was speculation that drugs played a role in his disappearance. However, no concrete evidence supported this theory.

3. Accidental Death: Another theory was that Brandon, disoriented and possibly injured, succumbed to the elements in the harsh Texas landscape.

Years passed with no significant developments until February 2022, when a search party found clothing near Brandon's last known location. Subsequent searches by the Texas Rangers uncovered human remains in the vicinity. While DNA testing was still ongoing at the time of discovery, Brandon's family accepted that the remains were likely his, given the proximity and context of the findings.

Despite the discovery of remains, the exact circumstances of Brandon's disappearance remain unclear. Some theories that have circulated include:

- Wild Animal Attack: The remote area where Brandon disappeared is home to various wildlife, including predators that could have attacked him if he was injured and unable to defend himself.

- Accidental Injury: Brandon mentioned he was bleeding during one of his calls to Kyle. It's possible he sustained an injury that incapacitated him, leading to his death from exposure or further injury.

- Human Foul Play: Though less supported by evidence, some believe that Brandon may have been a victim of foul play, possibly related to his drug use or the people he mentioned chasing him.

The disappearance of Brandon Lawson is a haunting case that highlights the difficulties in resolving missing person cases, particularly in remote and rugged terrains. The fragmentary evidence and the passage of time have only deepened the mystery. While the discovery of remains near his last known location has brought some measure of closure to his family, many questions remain unanswered.

As of now, the DNA analysis and investigation into Brandon's death are ongoing, with his family and the community holding out hope for definitive answers. The case underscores the importance of timely and thorough investigations, as well as the need for continued support for those left behind in the wake of such tragic disappearances.

Chapter Eleven

Raymond "RJ" McLeod

RAYMOND "RJ" McLeod, a former U.S. Marine and avid bodybuilder, became one of the U.S. Marshals Service's most wanted fugitives following the brutal murder of his girlfriend, Krystal Mitchell, in 2016. This chapter explores the details surrounding Krystal Mitchell's death, McLeod's subsequent flight from justice, and the extensive manhunt that ultimately led to his capture. The case highlights issues of domestic violence, international fugitive tracking, and the resilience of a victim's family in seeking justice.

* * *

Krystal Mitchell, a 30-year-old property manager from Phoenix, Arizona, met Raymond McLeod when he moved into the apartment complex she managed. The couple began dating, and after only a few weeks together, they decided to visit San Diego to see McLeod's friends. The trip, however, turned fatal.

On June 10, 2016, San Diego police responded to a 911 call reporting a woman not breathing in an apartment. Krystal Mitchell was found deceased with signs of a struggle; she had been brutally beaten and strangled. McLeod, who was the last person seen with her, had disappeared along with her car.

Following the discovery of Krystal's body, authorities quickly issued an arrest warrant for McLeod. Investigators believed he fled to Mexico shortly after the murder, driving Krystal's car to the San Diego airport, where he rented another vehicle to cross the border. This marked the beginning of an international manhunt.

Raymond McLeod's violent tendencies were well-documented. An ex-Marine with a history of heavy drinking, McLeod had been involved in multiple incidents of domestic violence. He had two ex-wives who both accused him of abuse, and one incident involved his roommate witnessing him strangling one of his wives. This history painted a grim picture of McLeod as a dangerous individual prone to violent outbursts.

McLeod's escape led him through several Central American countries. He was reportedly seen in Mexico, Guatemala, and Belize over the next few years. The U.S. Marshals Service, along with local authorities, pursued numerous leads, often narrowly missing him. His presence was confirmed in these countries through various sightings and tips, but he managed to evade capture, often disappearing just as authorities closed in.

Krystal Mitchell's mother, Josephine Funes Wentzel, played a crucial role in the search for McLeod. A former police detective, Wentzel utilized her investigative skills and social media to keep the public informed and to gather leads. She tirelessly campaigned for justice, traveling to Central America herself in hopes of finding McLeod. Her efforts brought significant attention to the case, ensuring it remained a priority for law enforcement.

In April 2021, McLeod was placed on the U.S.

Marshals' 15 Most Wanted list, the first fugitive to debut with an initial reward of $50,000 for information leading to his arrest. This unprecedented move high-lighted the danger McLeod posed and the urgency of capturing him. The reward and his placement on the list were widely publicized, furthering efforts to locate him.

After six years on the run, McLeod was finally captured on August 29, 2022, in Sonsonate, El Salvador. He was found living under an alias and was arrested by Salvadoran authorities in collaboration with the U.S. Marshals Service. McLeod's capture was a significant victory for law enforcement and a moment of profound relief for Krystal Mitchell's family.

Several theories and speculations arose during McLeod's time as a fugitive. His military background and survival skills likely aided him in evading capture for so long. Some believed he received help from individ-uals sympathetic to him or unaware of his true identity. His ability to blend into various communities and the transient lifestyle he adopted made tracking him extremely challenging.

The case of Raymond "RJ" McLeod underscores the complexities and challenges of capturing international fugitives. It also highlights the devastating impact of domestic violence and the importance of persistent and coordinated law enforcement efforts. Krystal Mitchell's tragic death and her family's unwavering quest for justice serve as a poignant reminder of the far-reaching consequences of violence and the resilience required to seek accountability. McLeod's capture brings a measure of closure, but the fight against domestic violence and the pursuit of justice for all victims continue.

Chapter Twelve

Patricia Meehan

PATRICIA BERNADETTE MEEHAN, a 37-year-old woman from Bozeman, Montana, disappeared on April 20, 1989, under circumstances that continue to baffle investigators and haunt her family. Known for her love of children and animals, Patricia was described as a gentle, kind-hearted person. Her mysterious disappearance followed a car accident on a remote highway in Montana and led to a series of reported sightings across several states, leaving behind a trail of questions and scant answers.

* * *

On the night of April 20, 1989, Patricia Meehan was driving on Highway 200 near Circle, Montana. Her car veered into the opposite lane, resulting in a head-on collision with another vehicle. The driver of the other car, Carol Heitz, was shaken but not seriously injured. Meehan, however, crawled out of her car, stared blankly at Heitz, and then walked away from the scene, climbing over a nearby fence and disappearing into the vast, desolate terrain of eastern Montana.

When law enforcement arrived, they found Meehan's car abandoned with her belongings inside. Given the remote location and the cold night, there was immediate concern for her well-being. Authorities launched an extensive search involving helicopters, bloodhounds, and ground teams, but despite their efforts, no trace of Patricia was found.

Patricia's family, Tom and Dolly Meehan, traveled from their home in Pennsylvania to Montana to assist with the search. They distributed thousands of flyers and spoke to locals, hoping to find someone who had seen their daughter. Their efforts, while heroic, yielded little in the way of concrete leads.

In the months following her disappearance, there were numerous reported sightings of Patricia Meehan across various states. Over 5,000 sightings were reported, with some appearing credible enough for the family and authorities to investigate further.

1. Luverne, Minnesota (May 4, 1989): A police officer spotted a woman resembling Patricia sitting in a Hardee's restaurant for over five hours, drinking water and appearing disoriented. When questioned, the woman claimed she was from Colorado and Israel and refused to give her name.

2. Sioux Falls, South Dakota (May 5, 1989): A waitress reported seeing a woman matching Patricia's description at a truck stop cafe. The woman stayed there for nearly 12 hours, drinking coffee and talking to herself.

3. Murdo, South Dakota (May 5, 1989): Another waitress saw a woman resembling Patricia with a man in his 30s at a local diner. The woman seemed out of place and distressed.

4. Bozeman, Montana (May 19, 1989): Patricia was reportedly seen at a diner in her hometown. She

appeared hurried and disoriented, asking to be served quickly as she had somewhere to be at 9 AM.

5. Tacoma, Washington (May 30, 1989): A truck driver saw a woman resembling Patricia on Interstate 90. She declined a ride, stating her car had broken down and she was looking for a phone.

These sightings created a pattern suggesting that Patricia might be hitchhiking across the country, possibly suffering from amnesia induced by the car accident.

Several theories have been proposed regarding Patricia Meehan's disappearance:

1. Amnesia: Many believe that Patricia suffered a head injury in the car accident, leading to memory loss and disorientation. This theory is supported by the behavior described in the sightings—Patricia often appeared confused and unsure of her identity.

2. Voluntary Disappearance: Some speculate that Patricia may have chosen to disappear intentionally due to psychological distress. She had been seeing a psychologist and was reportedly under significant stress prior to the accident.

3. Foul Play: There is possibility that Patricia encountered someone with malicious intent while

hitchhiking, leading to her abduction or murder. However, no evidence has been found to substantiate this theory.

4. Natural Causes: Another theory is that Patricia may have died from natural causes or an accident while wandering. If this were the case, she might have ended up as an unidentified decedent in another state.

The Meehan family remained steadfast in their search for Patricia. They traveled extensively, following up on reported sightings and appealing to the public for information. Their plight attracted media attention, and Patricia's case was featured on television shows such as "Unsolved Mysteries," which brought national awareness to her disappearance.

The family's determination and the widespread media coverage led to an influx of tips, but none provided the breakthrough they desperately needed. Despite the numerous reported sightings, each lead seemed to end in frustration and heartache.

Patricia Meehan's disappearance had a profound impact on her family and the community. Her case highlighted the challenges faced by families of missing persons and the often slow and bureaucratic nature of search and rescue operations. It also brought attention to the need for better support systems for individuals experiencing psychological distress.

Over the years, Patricia's case has remained open, with occasional new leads and sightings reported. Her family continues to hope for answers and remains vigilant in their quest to find her.

The disappearance of Patricia Meehan is a haunting and unresolved mystery. Despite the extensive search efforts, numerous reported sightings, and various theories, Patricia's fate remains unknown. Her case serves as a stark reminder of the many missing persons whose stories are left incomplete, their families yearning for closure and peace.

As the years pass, the hope of finding Patricia alive may fade, but the determination to uncover the truth endures. Her story is a testament to the resilience of the human spirit and the enduring bond of family love. It also underscores the importance of vigilance and empathy in the face of such tragic and mysterious events.

For anyone with information regarding Patricia Meehan's whereabouts, please contact the McCone County Sheriff's Office at 406-485-3405. Your tip could be the key to solving this enduring mystery.

Chapter Thirteen

Henry Hudson

THE STORY of Henry Hudson's disappearance is one of the most enigmatic and haunting tales from the Age of Exploration. As a daring navigator, Hudson's ambition to discover the Northwest Passage ultimately led to his mysterious and tragic end.

* * *

Henry Hudson was born around 1565 in England. Very little is known about his early life, but he emerged as a notable figure during the early 17th century due to his ambitious attempts to find new trade routes. He embarked on four major voyages, financed by both English and Dutch interests, with the goal of discovering a northerly route to Asia.

Hudson's fourth and final expedition began on April 17, 1610, when he set sail from London aboard the ship Discovery. This voyage was financed by the English and aimed once again at finding the elusive Northwest Passage to Asia. His crew consisted of experienced sailors, but the journey was fraught with challenges from the outset.

Hudson navigated through the icy waters of the North Atlantic, eventually reaching what is now known as the Hudson Strait and Hudson Bay. He believed he had found the passage, but as winter set in, the ship became trapped in ice in James Bay, Canada. The crew was forced to spend the winter there, enduring extreme cold and dwindling supplies.

By June 1611, tensions had reached a breaking point. The harsh winter, lack of food, and Hudson's decision to continue the expedition rather than return to

England led to unrest among the crew. On June 22, 1611, the situation escalated into mutiny. The mutineers, led by Robert Juet, Henry Greene, and others, seized control of the ship.

Hudson, along with his teenage son John and seven loyal crew members, were forced into a small open boat and set adrift. The Discovery sailed away, leaving Hudson and his companions to their fate in the unforgiving Arctic environment. The castaways were never seen again.

Upon the Discovery's return to England, the mutineers were arrested and charged with Hudson's murder. Despite the gravity of their actions, none were convicted. The lack of definitive evidence and the dire circumstances of the expedition contributed to their acquittal.

Historical accounts and documents from the trial provide some insights into the mutiny. Bloodstains and missing personal possessions of Hudson suggested foul play, but without bodies or direct witnesses to the final moments, the true nature of Hudson's end remains speculative.

Several theories have emerged over the centuries regarding Hudson's fate:

1. Death by Exposure: The most widely accepted theory is that Hudson and his companions succumbed to the elements. The Arctic environment, combined with their limited supplies, made survival unlikely. Historical accounts from the period highlight the harsh conditions they would have faced.

2. Murder by Crew: Some historians suggest that Hudson might have been killed outright by the mutineers before being set adrift. This theory is supported by the bloodstains found on the Discovery and the animosity that had built up among the crew during the harsh winter.

3. Survival and Assimilation: A more speculative theory posits that Hudson and the others might have survived and assimilated with local Indigenous populations. However, there is no concrete evidence to support this idea, and it remains in the realm of conjecture.

4. Cannibalism: Given the dire situation, some speculate that the castaways might have resorted to cannibalism in a desperate attempt to survive. This theory, while sensational, lacks any direct evidence.

Henry Hudson's legacy is profound despite his tragic end. His explorations significantly contributed to European knowledge of the North American coastline and the Arctic regions. The Hudson River, Hudson Strait, and Hudson Bay all bear his name, commemorating his contributions to navigation and exploration.

His disappearance remains one of the great unsolved mysteries of the Age of Exploration, a poignant reminder of the perilous nature of early voyages and the human cost of these daring enterprises.

The disappearance of Henry Hudson is a story of ambition, exploration, and human endurance. While the exact details of his fate may never be known, his impact on the world of exploration is undeniable. Hudson's story continues to captivate historians and adventurers alike, symbolizing the relentless quest for discovery and the enduring mysteries of the past.

Chapter Fourteen

Ruth Wilson

On November 27, 1995, Ruth Wilson, a 16-year-old schoolgirl from Betchworth, Surrey, disappeared under enigmatic circumstances. Despite extensive searches and investigations, her fate remains unknown.

* * *

Ruth Wilson's day started like any other. She had no morning lessons and remained at home until 11:30 AM, when she took a taxi to Dorking. Her journey was uneventful until she made a seemingly routine stop at Thistles Florists on Dorking High Street around noon, where she ordered a bouquet of flowers to be delivered to her stepmother on November 29.

After the florist visit, Ruth spent the afternoon at the local library. Around 4:00 PM, she took another taxi to Box Hill, a scenic beauty spot. The taxi driver who dropped her off reported that Ruth stood still in the rain, not moving from the spot where she was dropped off. This unusual behavior would later contribute to various theories about her disappearance.

When Ruth did not return home that evening, her parents, Ian and Karen Wilson, became concerned. They contacted her school and discovered she had not attended classes that day. The police were informed, and an initial search was conducted in the immediate area of Box Hill. This search included police dogs, helicopters, and thermal imaging equipment, but yielded no significant clues.

In the days following Ruth's disappearance, her parents received the flowers she had ordered, but there was no note attached. On December 1, police discovered three notes hidden under a bush in the undergrowth at Betchworth Quarry on Box Hill. The notes, confirmed to be in Ruth's handwriting, were farewells addressed to her father, stepmother, best friend, and a teenage boy. Nearby, empty packets of paracetamol tablets and a half-empty bottle of Vermouth were found, suggesting a possible suicide attempt.

However, no body was found, leading to speculation that Ruth might still be alive. This theory was supported by the lack of any definitive evidence pointing to her death at the scene.

The Surrey Police launched an extensive investigation, known as Operation Scholar. Despite the initial searches, no concrete evidence was found to indicate what had happened to Ruth. The case garnered significant media attention, with Ruth's parents making public appeals for information.

Several eyewitnesses came forward with reports of sightings. A year after her disappearance, a girl resembling Ruth was seen at a newsagent's shop in Dorking, appearing distressed and upset when she could not get a copy of a local newspaper. This encounter was captured on CCTV, but the identity of the girl remains unconfirmed.

Additionally, Ruth's friend, Catherine Mair, described Ruth as being unhappy at home and tight-lipped about her troubles. This insight fueled theories that Ruth might have run away to escape personal issues.

Theories and Speculations

1. Suicide: The discovery of the notes and the items found near Betchworth Quarry initially suggested a suicide attempt. However, the absence of a body and other corroborating evidence left this theory inconclusive.

2. Abduction or Murder: Some theories propose that Ruth might have been abducted or met with foul play. However, extensive searches and investigations did not uncover any evidence supporting this theory. Mark Williams-Thomas, the family liaison officer, suggested that Ruth might have gone to meet someone and subsequently left, or that she might have died by other means.

3. Voluntary Disappearance: Another theory is that Ruth ran away voluntarily. Her unhappiness at home and the farewell notes support this possibility. However, disappearing without a trace is challenging,

especially for a young girl without significant resources.

The case remains open, with periodic reviews by the Surrey Police. The Wilson family continues to hope for answers and believes that Ruth might still be alive. Over the years, various appeals for information have been made through media outlets, but no new substantial leads have emerged.

Despite the passage of time, Ruth Wilson's disappearance remains one of the most baffling cases in the UK. Her story continues to intrigue and haunt those who follow unsolved mysteries, with each theory leaving more questions than answers.

Her family's determination to find her and the community's support reflect a collective hope that someday, the truth will emerge, and Ruth's story will finally have a resolution.

Chapter Fifteen

David Guerrero

DAVID GUERRERO GUEVARA, affectionately known as
"El Niño Pintor" (The Little Painter), was a prodigious
young artist from Málaga, Spain. Born on October 19,
1973, David displayed exceptional talent in painting
from a very young age. On April 6, 1987, at the age of

13, David disappeared under mysterious circumstances, leaving behind a legacy of unanswered questions and a family grappling with grief and uncertainty.

* * *

David was preparing for his first major art exhibition at the prestigious La Maison art gallery in Málaga. His painting, a depiction of "Cristo de la Buena Muerte," had received critical acclaim, and a local journalist had expressed interest in interviewing him about his work. David, who was known to be shy and somewhat nervous about the attention, mentioned feeling anxious about the upcoming interview and exhibition.

On the afternoon of April 6, 1987, David returned home from school, changed his clothes, and prepared to leave for the art gallery. He was supposed to take a bus to La Maison, located a short distance from his home. His mother, Antonia Guevara, watched him leave the house at around 6:30 PM, noting that he appeared calm despite his earlier nervousness.

David never made it to the gallery. When his father, José Guevara, arrived at the art academy to pick him up later that evening, he was alarmed to find that David had never arrived. The family immediately reported his disappearance to the police, sparking a massive search effort across Málaga.

The initial police response was thorough but ultimately fruitless. Investigators conducted extensive searches in and around Málaga, interviewing friends, family, and anyone who might have seen David on the day of his disappearance. Despite these efforts, no significant leads emerged in the early days of the investigation.

Eyewitness Accounts:

1. The Swiss Suspect: In the months following David's disappearance, a peculiar clue emerged. A hotel maid found a napkin with David's full name written on it in a room previously occupied by a 70-year-old Swiss man. This man, described as wealthy and interested in photography, had been staying in Málaga during the time of David's disappearance. Despite the promising lead, the man had died in 1990 before the police could thoroughly investigate him. Some of David's last drawings bore a resemblance to this man, adding to the suspicion.

2. Anonymous Tips and New Leads: Over the years, several anonymous tips have been received. One notable tip implicated a man named Gervasio, who was allegedly associated with the Peña El Cenachero, the art academy where David was taking

classes. This lead, along with sightings of David in various locations such as Lisbon and other parts of Europe, kept the investigation alive, though no concrete evidence was ever found to substantiate these claims.

3. David's Art and Possible Motives: Some theories suggest that David's artistic talent may have played a role in his disappearance. One hypothesis posits that he was targeted by a network involved in art forgery or exploitation, recognizing his potential value. Alternatively, some speculate that envy or jealousy within his circle could have led to foul play.

David's disappearance deeply affected his family and the local community. His mother, Antonia, kept a light on and the front door ajar every night, hoping for his return. The case, while officially closed in 1996 due to the lack of new leads and the statute of limitations on possible crimes, was never forgotten by the authorities or his family.

In 2018, David's surviving family members organized an art exhibition to honor his memory and showcase his works. This event served both as a tribute to David's talent and a reminder of the ongoing mystery surrounding his disappearance.

In recent years, renewed efforts have been made to

revisit the case. The National Police of Spain re-examined the files with the help of modern forensic techniques and new investigative perspectives. Although no new evidence has definitively solved the case, the continued interest and occasional new tips provide a glimmer of hope for closure.

The case of David Guerrero Guevara has spawned numerous theories, each as intriguing and troubling as the next. Here are some of the most discussed:

1. Kidnapping by a Stranger: The most straightforward theory is that David was abducted by someone he did not know. The Swiss suspect remains a focal point for many who believe that his mysterious presence and the napkin clue are too coincidental to ignore.

2. Artistic Exploitation: Given David's talent, some believe he may have been lured by someone who wanted to exploit his skills for financial gain. This theory is supported by the idea that he could have been taken by an art forgery ring or other criminal organization interested in his unique abilities.

3. Local Foul Play: Another theory is that David fell victim to someone within his own community, possibly motivated by jealousy or other personal reasons. The involvement of individuals from the

Peña El Cenachero, as suggested by some tips, points to this possibility.

4. Human Trafficking: Some have speculated that David might have been abducted for the purpose of human trafficking. While there is no direct evidence to support this theory, the general vulnerability of young children to such crimes makes it a consideration in many missing persons cases.

David's disappearance had a profound impact on his family and the community of Málaga. His father, José, who passed away in 2015, never ceased in his efforts to find his son. The emotional toll on his mother, Antonia, and his siblings has been immense. The local community also felt the loss deeply, as David's talent and potential had made him a beloved figure in the neighborhood.

In 2019, a significant event reignited public interest in the case: a classmate of David's found a drawing in her mailbox, one that David had given her shortly before his disappearance. This drawing, believed to be the original, had previously been turned over to the police. Its mysterious reappearance raised questions about whether someone was still trying to communicate clues about David's fate.

* * *

The disappearance of David Guerrero Guevara remains one of Spain's most enduring and unsettling mysteries. Despite decades of investigation, countless hours of searching, and the unyielding hope of his family, the truth about what happened to David continues to elude everyone involved.

The case stands as a poignant reminder of the pain and uncertainty that families of missing persons endure. It also underscores the importance of keeping such cases in the public eye, as any new piece of information could potentially unlock the mystery and bring long-awaited answers.

David Guerrero Guevara's legacy lives on through his art and the memories of those who knew and loved him. The search for answers continues, driven by the enduring hope that one day, the mystery of "El Niño Pintor" will finally be resolved.

Chapter Sixteen

Lauren Spierer

LAUREN SPIERER, a 20-year-old Indiana University student, vanished in the early hours of June 3, 2011, after a night out with friends in Bloomington, Indiana.

Her disappearance has remained a haunting mystery, sparking extensive investigations, numerous theories, and continued media attention.

* * *

Lauren Spierer, originally from Scarsdale, New York, was a sophomore studying fashion at Indiana University. On the night of June 2, 2011, Lauren joined friends at her apartment to watch a basketball game before heading out for a night of partying. Among her companions were Jason Rosenbaum and Corey Rossman, friends she had met through her boyfriend, Jesse Wolff.

Around 12:30 AM, Lauren left her apartment and headed to a party at Rosenbaum's townhouse. The group consumed alcohol, and it is speculated that drugs such as Klonopin and cocaine were also involved. Surveillance footage captured Lauren leaving her apartment, looking happy and well.

After the party, Lauren and Rossman went to Kilroy's Sports Bar, where they stayed for about 30 minutes. Notably, Lauren left her cell phone and shoes at the bar. The pair then headed back to her apartment complex, Smallwood Plaza. There, they encountered a group of young men, one of whom punched Rossman, causing him to lose much of his memory of the night.

Following the altercation, surveillance footage showed Rossman carrying an intoxicated Lauren over his shoulder as they left the apartment complex. They arrived at Rossman's apartment, where he allegedly vomited and went to bed. Lauren then went next door to Rosenbaum's apartment. Rosenbaum insisted Lauren sleep on his couch, but she refused and left around 4:30 AM, intending to return to her apartment. This was the last confirmed sighting of Lauren Spierer.

Lauren's disappearance prompted a massive search effort involving local police, the FBI, and volunteers. Investigators scoured Bloomington and its surroundings, utilizing dogs, divers, and aerial searches. Despite these efforts, no trace of Lauren was found.

Key individuals from that night, including Rossman, Rosenbaum, Michael Beth (Rossman's roommate), and Jesse Wolff, were all interviewed by police. They were considered persons of interest but not suspects. While they cooperated with the investigation, some took independent polygraphs instead of police-administered ones, leading to criticism from Lauren's family.

Several theories have emerged regarding Lauren Spierer's disappearance:

1. Accidental Overdose: Given Lauren's level of intoxication and her possible use of drugs, one theory

suggests she may have overdosed. Some speculate that her friends, fearing legal consequences, may have hidden her body. However, private investigator Bo Dietl, hired by the Spierer family, doubts that a fatal drug overdose would have prompted such actions, citing the commonality of drug use on campus.

2. Stranger Abduction: Another theory is that Lauren was abducted by a stranger as she walked home alone in an intoxicated state. Given her small stature and the fact that she was barefoot, it is plausible that someone could have easily overpowered her. Police have not ruled out this possibility, though Lauren's parents believe someone she knew was involved.

3. Foul Play by Acquaintances: Lauren's parents have expressed suspicion towards the friends she was with that night, believing they know more than they have revealed. Civil lawsuits were filed against Rossman, Rosenbaum, and Beth, accusing them of negligence in ensuring Lauren's safety. These suits were eventually dismissed due to lack of evidence proving their direct involvement in her disappearance.

4. Daniel Messel: In 2017, Brown County prosecutor Ted Adams suggested a potential connection between Lauren's case and Daniel Messel, convicted of killing IU student Hannah Wilson in 2015.

However, no charges have been brought against Messel in connection with Lauren's disappearance.

The Spierer family has continued to search for answers, utilizing private investigators and maintaining public awareness through media and social media campaigns. The case has been featured in various true crime shows and podcasts, keeping it in the public eye.

* * *

The disappearance of Lauren Spierer remains an unresolved mystery, leaving her family and friends in a state of perpetual grief and uncertainty. Despite extensive investigations and widespread media coverage, the case has yielded few concrete answers. Lauren's story serves as a sobering reminder of the vulnerabilities young adults can face and the enduring pain of not knowing the fate of a loved one.

Her disappearance is a call to action for better safety measures and support systems for students and young adults. As the years pass, the hope for closure remains, driven by the relentless pursuit of truth by those who knew and loved Lauren.

Chapter Seventeen

George Mallory

GEORGE MALLORY, an English mountaineer, became a legendary figure in the annals of exploration due to his attempts to summit Mount Everest in the early 1920s. His enigmatic disappearance during a 1924 expedition, alongside his climbing partner Andrew Irvine, has fascinated and puzzled historians, climbers, and the public for decades.

Mallory's involvement with Everest began in 1921 when he joined the British reconnaissance expedition to identify potential routes to the summit. Despite severe challenges, including altitude sickness and exhaustion, the team succeeded in mapping out a feasible path. Mallory returned in 1922, attempting to reach the summit but was thwarted by an avalanche and severe weather conditions.

By 1924, at the age of 37, Mallory was acutely aware that this might be his last opportunity to conquer Everest. The third British Everest expedition set out with renewed determination, hoping to achieve what had so far eluded them.

The 1924 expedition reached Everest in early May. By late May, they had established several camps, with Camp IV positioned on the North Col at over 23,000 feet. Mallory and Irvine, equipped with oxygen apparatus, set off from Camp IV on June 6, aiming for the summit.

On June 8, 1924, fellow climbers Noel Odell reported seeing Mallory and Irvine ascending the northeast ridge, approximately 800 feet below the summit, before clouds obscured his view. This was the last confirmed sighting of the pair. When they failed to return, a search was conducted, but no trace of them was found.

Initial search efforts were limited by the harsh conditions and the technology of the time. The first significant clue emerged in 1933 when Percy Wyn-Harris discovered an ice axe believed to belong to Irvine near the First Step on the northeast ridge. This finding spurred further interest but provided no definitive answers.

In 1975, Chinese climber Wang Hongbao reported seeing a body, which he described as an "English dead," but his account was not followed up until much later due to political and logistical challenges.

The mystery surrounding Mallory's disappearance persisted until 1999, when the Mallory and Irvine Research Expedition set out to locate the climbers' remains. Using clues from previous expeditions, including Wang's report, the team focused their search on the northeast ridge.

On May 1, 1999, Conrad Anker discovered Mallory's body at an altitude of 26,760 feet. The body was remarkably well-preserved due to the cold, dry conditions. Mallory's torso was found in a self-arrest position, suggesting he had attempted to stop a fall. His injuries indicated he had suffered a severe fall, likely causing his death. However, the position of his body and the absence of Irvine's remains or the camera they carried left many questions unanswered.

Several theories have emerged regarding the fate of Mallory and Irvine:

1. Summit Success: One of the most compelling theories is that Mallory and Irvine might have reached the summit before their fatal fall. This theory hinges on the possibility that Irvine's camera, if found, could contain photographic evidence of their achievement. However, despite numerous search efforts, the camera has never been located.

2. Accidental Fall: The discovery of Mallory's body and the nature of his injuries support the theory that he fell to his death. The position of his body and

the rope injuries suggest that he and Irvine were roped together when one of them fell, pulling the other down. The ice axe found in 1933 and other personal items scattered along the ridge indicate a tragic accident.

3. Hypoxia and Exhaustion: Climbing at such altitudes without modern oxygen equipment is perilous. It is possible that Mallory and Irvine succumbed to hypoxia (lack of oxygen) and exhaustion, leading to disorientation and a fatal misstep.

4. Mysterious Interventions: Over the years, various unsubstantiated theories have suggested foul play or intervention by other climbers, but these remain speculative without concrete evidence.

George Mallory's disappearance and the subsequent discovery of his body have cemented his status as a romantic and tragic figure in the history of exploration. His famous response to why he wanted to climb Everest, "Because it's there," has become emblematic of the spirit of adventure and human determination.

Mallory's letters, including those found with his body, reveal a man acutely aware of the risks he faced but driven by an unyielding desire to achieve greatness. His correspondence with his wife, Ruth, published posthumously, provides a poignant insight into his thoughts and emotions during the final days of his life.

* * *

The disappearance of George Mallory on Mount Everest remains one of the most intriguing mysteries in the history of mountaineering. While the discovery of his body in 1999 provided some answers, many questions about his final moments and whether he reached the summit before his death remain unanswered. Mallory's legacy endures, inspiring generations of climbers and adventurers drawn to the formidable challenge of Everest and the indomitable human spirit.

Chapter Eighteen

David Sneddon

DAVID LOUIS SNEDDON was a bright and adventurous 24-year-old student from Brigham Young University (BYU) who disappeared while hiking in Yunnan Province, China, in August 2004. His case remains one of the most perplexing disappearances involving a foreign national in recent history.

* * *

David Sneddon was the youngest of eleven children in a close-knit family. He grew up in Nebraska, where he developed a love for the outdoors, musicals, and sports. An Eagle Scout, David was known for his adventurous spirit and strong sense of responsibility. He attended BYU, where he majored in Asian studies and was fluent in both Korean and Mandarin Chinese. David's passion for Asian cultures was further fueled by his missionary service in South Korea, where he developed a deep appreciation for the region and its people.

In the summer of 2004, David traveled to China to improve his Mandarin and explore the country. On August 14, 2004, he set off on a solo hike through Tiger Leaping Gorge, a scenic and treacherous canyon along the Jinsha River. David's family last heard from him through an email sent from Lijiang, where he mentioned his plans to hike the gorge before returning to Beijing.

David was last seen leaving a Korean restaurant in the town of Shangri-La on August 14, 2004. He failed to meet his brother at the Seoul airport as planned, prompting immediate concern. When David did not show up, his family reported him missing, and an extensive search was launched.

Chinese authorities initially suggested that David had likely fallen into the Jinsha River and drowned. The U.S. State Department concurred with this assessment, concluding that it was a tragic accident. However, David's family was skeptical of this explanation. They knew David to be a skilled and cautious hiker, and they were troubled by the lack of physical evidence, such as his body or personal belongings, being found in or near the river.

David's father, Roy, and his brothers, Michael and James, traveled to China to conduct their own search. They trekked through Tiger Leaping Gorge and spoke with locals and hikers, but found no trace of David. They also discovered that the hiking trail was situated far from the river, making it unlikely that David could have fallen in by accident. Additionally, they encountered several people who claimed to have seen David after he supposedly completed the hike.

Multiple eyewitnesses reported seeing David after his disappearance, which further fueled the family's doubts about the drowning theory. A café owner in the mountain region described a young man matching David's description who spoke fluent Korean. She recalled him visiting her café multiple times before telling her he was leaving. This account suggested that

David had not only survived the hike but was making plans to continue his travels.

Years later, new information emerged from Japanese sources suggesting that David had been spotted in North Korea, where he was reportedly teaching English. This claim, though unverified, added a new and disturbing dimension to the case.

Over the years, a compelling theory has gained traction: David Sneddon may have been abducted by North Korean agents. This theory is rooted in North Korea's known history of abducting foreign nationals to use as language instructors for their intelligence agents. The regime has admitted to kidnapping numerous Japanese citizens for this purpose, and it is believed that nationals from other countries, including South Korea and Thailand, have also been taken.

Several factors support the abduction theory in David's case. Firstly, his fluency in Korean and Mandarin made him an ideal target for North Korean operatives seeking language instructors. Secondly, the lack of any physical evidence of an accident in Tiger Leaping Gorge casts doubt on the initial conclusion of drowning. Lastly, the sightings of David in North Korea, though unconfirmed, align with known patterns of North Korean abductions.

David's family has never given up hope of finding

him. They have worked tirelessly to raise awareness about his case and advocate for a thorough investigation. They have reached out to U.S. government officials, international organizations, and media outlets to keep David's story in the public eye. Their efforts have led to resolutions in the U.S. Congress urging further investigation into David's disappearance and potential abduction by North Korea.

In 2016, new reports surfaced suggesting that David was alive in North Korea, where he had started a family. These reports, based on information from Japanese sources, provided a glimmer of hope to the Sneddon family and renewed calls for action. U.S. officials have expressed concern and pledged to investigate these claims, but concrete evidence remains elusive.

* * *

The disappearance of David Sneddon remains an unsolved mystery, with his family continuing to search for answers. Whether he met with an unfortunate accident in China or was abducted by North Korean agents, David's case highlights the complexities and challenges of international disappearances.

David Sneddon's case also serves as a reminder of the broader issue of North Korean abductions and the need for international cooperation to address these human rights violations. As the search for David continues, his family and supporters remain committed to uncovering the truth and ensuring that he is not forgotten.

Chapter Nineteen

Leah Roberts

LEAH TOBY ROBERTS, a 23-year-old college student from North Carolina, disappeared in March 2000 during a cross-country road trip. Her case has intrigued and baffled investigators, family, and true crime enthusiasts for over two decades. Despite numerous leads and extensive investigations, her whereabouts remain unknown.

* * *

Leah was born on July 23, 1976, in Durham, North Carolina. Her early life was marked by tragedy: her father, Stancil Roberts, was diagnosed with a chronic lung disease, and her mother, Nancy, died suddenly of heart failure while Leah was still in college. These events profoundly impacted Leah, leading her to take time off from North Carolina State University, where she was studying anthropology and Spanish.

In 1998, Leah survived a severe car accident that resulted in a punctured lung and a shattered femur, which required a metal rod to be implanted in her leg. This near-death experience, combined with the loss of her parents, prompted Leah to seek a deeper meaning in life. She became fascinated with the works of Jack Kerouac, particularly "On the Road" and "The Dharma Bums," which inspired her desire for a spiritual and physical journey.

On March 9, 2000, Leah abruptly decided to embark on a road trip without informing her friends or family. She left a note for her roommate, Nicole, explaining that she needed some time away and assuring her that she was not suicidal. Leah withdrew a significant amount of cash from her bank account and packed her 1993 white Jeep Cherokee with personal belongings, including her cat, Bea.

Leah's journey took her across several states. Her debit card records showed purchases of gas and motel stays along Interstate 40, indicating she was heading west. The last known use of her debit card was at a gas station in Brooks, Oregon, on March 13, 2000. Surveillance footage from the station showed Leah alone and seemingly in good spirits.

On March 18, 2000, joggers in the Mount Baker-Snoqualmie National Forest in Washington state discovered Leah's Jeep Cherokee at the bottom of a steep embankment along Canyon Creek Road. The vehicle had apparently careened off the road, rolling several times before coming to a stop. Inside the Jeep, investigators found Leah's personal items, including her passport, checkbook, clothing, and $2,400 in cash. The vehicle's windows were covered with blankets, suggesting it might have been used as a shelter.

There were no signs of Leah at the crash site, and the lack of blood or any indications of injury led investigators to suspect that she was not in the vehicle at the time of the crash. Additionally, a wire under the car's hood had been cut, allowing the Jeep to accelerate without a driver, which further suggested that the crash might have been staged.

Leah's siblings, Kara and Heath Roberts, flew to Washington to assist in the search. They distributed flyers and spoke to locals, hoping to find someone who had seen Leah. Several witnesses came forward with possible sightings. Two men claimed to have met Leah at a restaurant in Bellingham, Washington, on March 13. They said she had discussed her road trip and her admiration for Kerouac. One of the men reported that Leah left the restaurant with another man, who was later referred to as "Barry." However, no other witnesses could corroborate this sighting, and the identity of "Barry" remains unknown.

A week after the discovery of Leah's Jeep, an anonymous tipster called the Whatcom County Sheriff's Office, claiming to have seen Leah at a Texaco gas station in Everett, Washington. The caller described her as appearing disoriented but hung up before providing further details.

Several theories have emerged over the years regarding Leah's disappearance:

1. Voluntary Disappearance: Some believe that Leah, inspired by Kerouac's philosophy, chose to disappear

voluntarily to start a new life. Her note and the withdrawn cash suggest she planned to be away for an extended period. However, her family and friends argue that Leah would not have left without eventually contacting them.

2. Abduction: Given the mysterious circumstances and the anonymous tipster's report, it is possible that Leah was abducted. The staged crash and the absence of any signs of struggle at the scene lend some credence to this theory. However, no solid evidence has been found to support it.

3. Accidental Death: Another theory is that Leah may have met with an accident or succumbed to the elements while wandering in the forest. The lack of blood or injuries in the Jeep makes this less likely, but it remains a possibility given the remote location where her vehicle was found.

4. Foul Play by "Barry": The man known as "Barry" mentioned in the restaurant account has never been identified or located. Some speculate that he may have had a role in Leah's disappearance, but without corroborating witnesses or evidence, this theory remains speculative.

Despite extensive searches by law enforcement, private investigators, and volunteers, Leah Roberts remains missing. In 2006, the case was revisited by new detectives who discovered a male DNA sample on one of her belongings, but it has not led to any significant breakthroughs.

Leah's family continues to hold out hope for answers. They have appeared on various television shows and maintained a website dedicated to finding Leah, urging anyone with information to come forward. The case remains open, with the Whatcom County Sheriff's Office periodically reviewing new tips and leads.

* * *

The disappearance of Leah Roberts is a haunting mystery that continues to perplex investigators and deeply affect her family and friends. Her story is a poignant reminder of the uncertainties and dangers that can accompany the search for meaning and adventure. As the years pass, the hope for finding Leah may dwindle, but the quest for answers and the pursuit of truth persist, driven by the enduring love and determination of those who knew her.

Chapter Twenty

Kris Kremers and Lisanne Froon

ON APRIL 1, 2014, two Dutch students, Kris Kremers and Lisanne Froon, vanished while hiking near Boquete, Panama. Their disappearance has become one of the most baffling and haunting mysteries of the 21st century.

* * *

Kris Kremers, 21, and Lisanne Froon, 22, were friends who decided to take a trip to Panama as a break before continuing their studies. They arrived in Boquete on March 29, 2014, staying with a local host family. Their plan was to explore the area and participate in volunteer work, which unfortunately fell through due to administrative miscommunications.

On April 1, 2014, Kris and Lisanne embarked on a hike along the Pianista Trail, a popular route leading to the Continental Divide. The women left their host family's home around 11:00 AM, equipped with a backpack containing essentials like a camera, phones, and a water bottle. Eyewitnesses reported seeing them on the trail with a local dog, which later returned home alone, raising the first alarm.

When the women did not return by evening, their host family grew concerned. On April 2, the parents of the girls were notified, and the search began. Unfortunately, initial search efforts were delayed due to miscommunication and a lack of urgency from local authorities. By April 6, the parents of Kris and Lisanne arrived in Panama, along with Dutch detectives to assist in the search.

On June 14, 2014, a local woman found a backpack

belonging to Lisanne Froon on the banks of a river near the village of Alto Romero, several kilometers from the Pianista Trail. The backpack contained both women's phones, a camera, two bras, a water bottle, and $83 in cash. Remarkably, the electronics were dry and in good condition despite being in the rainforest for weeks.

Forensic analysis of the phones revealed a series of attempted emergency calls starting just hours after the hike began. The first distress call was made at 4:39 PM on April 1 from Kris's iPhone, but due to poor reception, none of the calls went through. Over the next several days, multiple attempts were made to dial emergency numbers from both phones, but all failed to connect.

The camera provided further insights into their ordeal. The last daylight photos were taken on April 1, showing the women smiling and in good spirits on the trail. Disturbingly, the camera also contained 90 night-time photos taken between April 8 and 11, mostly of dark, blurry images with a few showing close-up details of rocks and possibly their belongings. The exact purpose of these photos remains unclear, though it is speculated they were trying to use the flash to signal for help or light their way.

In the weeks following the backpack's discovery, various bone fragments were found along the same river. Forensic testing confirmed they belonged to Kris and Lisanne. Lisanne's bones appeared to be naturally decomposed, while some of Kris's bones showed signs of being bleached, which raised numerous questions and speculations.

The investigation into the disappearance of Kris Kremers and Lisanne Froon was extensive and complex, involving multiple agencies and various lines of inquiry:

1. Search Efforts: The initial search efforts involved local indigenous tribes, police, and later, Dutch search and rescue teams. The terrain of the Pianista Trail and surrounding jungle made the search challenging. Despite extensive ground searches, air reconnaissance, and river patrols, the dense jungle and rugged landscape impeded efforts.

2. Forensic Analysis: The analysis of the phones and camera provided critical, albeit incomplete, insights. The detailed log of emergency call attempts indicated the women had been alive for at least several days after their disappearance. The camera's photos, particularly those taken at night, suggested they were disoriented and possibly injured.

3. Local Cooperation and Suspicion: The involvement of local guides and residents was both a help and a hindrance. Some locals provided valuable assistance, while others were suspected of withholding information or potentially being involved. One guide, in particular, was scrutinized for his inconsistent statements and suspicious behavior.

4. Geographic Information: The location of the remains and personal items suggested the women had ventured far off the trail. The discovery of Lisanne's backpack and Kris's bones miles apart raised questions

about how they had traveled such a distance, whether due to disorientation, injury, or external factors.

Eyewitness reports and discovered items provided fragmented but crucial clues:

1. Host Family and Locals: The host family reported the women had planned to hike but expressed concern when the dog returned without them. Locals reported seeing the women on the trail, but no confirmed sightings were made after the afternoon of April 1.

2. Timeline Discrepancies: The precise timeline of events was difficult to establish due to gaps in data and the remote, rugged environment. The photos taken near the Mirador (viewpoint) on April 1 indicated they reached the summit, but subsequent photos and emergency call attempts suggested they became lost or injured soon after.

3. Unusual Findings: The condition of the found items, particularly the phones and camera, suggested they had not been exposed to the elements for the entire duration. The presence of unknown fingerprints on the recovered items also raised suspicions of third-party involvement.

Several theories have been proposed to explain the tragic fate of Kris Kremers and Lisanne Froon:

1. Accidental Death: The official stance of Panamanian authorities is that the women got lost, suffered injuries, and eventually succumbed to the elements. The evidence of numerous emergency call attempts and the timeline of photos support this theory. They may have fallen into a ravine, with Kris possibly dying first, leading Lisanne to use the phone and camera in desperation.

2. Foul Play: The deletion of photo 509 and the presence of unknown fingerprints on the recovered items have led some to suspect foul play. The condition of the bones and the fact that Kris's remains were partially bleached have fueled these suspicions. Some theorize that a third party may have been involved, either directly causing their deaths or finding and altering the remains posthumously.

3. Human Trafficking or Murder: Some believe the women may have encountered criminal elements in the region, possibly linked to human trafficking or drug cartels. The area around Boquete is known for its remoteness and potential dangers, including wildlife and unscrupulous individuals.

4. Local Involvement: Certain locals, including

guides and residents, came under suspicion due to their behavior and statements. One guide's involvement, in particular, was scrutinized, as he had been one of the last people to see the women and had access to the area where their remains were found.

* * *

The disappearance and subsequent death of Kris Kremers and Lisanne Froon is a heartbreaking and complex case that has left many questions unanswered. Despite extensive searches and investigations, the exact circumstances of their demise remain shrouded in mystery. The recovered photos and phone data provide a fragmented narrative, but the truth of what happened in the Panamanian jungle may never be fully known. Their story serves as a tragic reminder of the potential dangers that can befall even the most prepared travelers.

Author's Excerpt

Conspiracy Theories That Were True

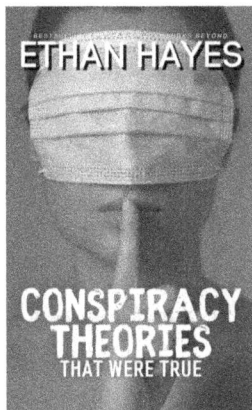

MK-ULTRA

Project MK-ULTRA, also called the CIA mind control program, was the code name given to an illegal and clandestine program of experiments on human subjects. It was designed and undertaken by the U.S. Central Intelligence Agency (CIA) in the 1950s and 1960s. MK-ULTRA was initiated in response to perceived threats from enemy forces, especially during the Cold War. The U.S. intelligence community believed that adversaries like the Soviet Union might be using mind control techniques, so MK-ULTRA was launched to develop their own potential methods for mind control.

* * *

ORIGINS:

During the Korean War (1950-1953), there were reports of American prisoners of war (POWs) confessing to using biological weapons — allegations that were largely seen as false by U.S. authorities. These confessions and the behavior of some returning POWs raised fears of "brainwashing" techniques being employed by Communist forces.

The U.S. intelligence community became interested in the potential use of mind-altering substances as tools for interrogation, mind control, and even the manipulation of foreign leaders. This interest was heightened by reports that Soviet, Chinese, and North Korean agents were using drugs to manipulate individuals and extract information.

Officially sanctioned in 1953 by CIA Director Allen Dulles and absorbed earlier covert operations such as Project BLUEBIRD (later renamed ARTICHOKE) that aimed at discovering methods of controlling the human mind. These operations experimented with hypnosis, forced addiction, and the use of drugs like sodium amytal. MK-ULTRA expanded on the previous projects.

THE EXPERIMENTS:

MK-ULTRA involved various experiments, many of which were carried out without the knowledge or consent of the subjects. The program's focus was broad, encompassing efforts to identify drugs or techniques that could be used for mind control, information extraction, influencing foreign leaders, or even altering an individual's personality. Some of the most notable aspects and experiments under MK-ULTRA include:

- **LSD Experiments**: Unwitting subjects: The CIA administered LSD to numerous individuals without their knowledge or consent, hoping to discover a "truth serum." This included both civilians and government employees. Some of these experiments took place in safe houses in San Francisco and

New York City, where the CIA would lure subjects with prostitutes and then dose them with the drug.

- **Effects on mental health**: Dr. Frank Olson, a biological warfare expert, was covertly dosed with LSD. Nine days later, he died in what was described as a suicide, jumping from a hotel window. The circumstances of his death remain controversial.

- **Use of Other Drugs**: LSD was the most researched substance, but the CIA also experimented with other drugs, including amphetamines, barbiturates, and mescaline. These were often combined to study their synergistic effects.

- **Hypnosis**: There were attempts to induce hypnosis to create "couriers" who could deliver messages without being aware of their content or "assassins" who would carry out orders without recalling them. These goals were in line with creating a 'Manchurian Candidate'-type individual (referring to the novel and film where a person is brainwashed into becoming an unwitting assassin).

- **Subproject 68**: Led by Dr. Ewen Cameron at the Allan Memorial Institute in Canada, this infamous project involved "depatterning" and "psychic driving." Patients were exposed to repeated, high-dose electroshock treatments and prolonged drug-induced sleep, followed by forced listening to taped messages for days on end. The intent was to "wipe" a person's memories and personality and then "reprogram" them. Many patients suffered severe long-term damage.

- **Magic Mushrooms (Psilocybin)**: The CIA was interested in the potential uses of psilocybin, the active ingredient in magic mushrooms. Dr. James C. Ketchum conducted experiments with the drug on soldiers at Edgewood Arsenal in Maryland.

- **Chemical, Biological, and Radiological Experiments**: While drug experiments are the most well-known aspect of MK-ULTRA, the program also included studies on the use of biological agents and toxins, as well as radiation exposure.

- **Institutional Involvement**: Research often took place in prestigious institutions. Some of the institutions were aware of the CIA's involvement, but many were not, with funding being channeled through front organizations. This included universities, hospitals, and pharmaceutical companies.
- **Safehouses and Surveillance**: In the 1950s and 1960s, the CIA operated safehouses in the U.S., especially in San Francisco and New York. These were used for LSD experiments and to study sexual blackmail and surveillance technology.

The effects of these experiments varied widely. Some subjects experienced mere confusion or short-term anxiety, while others suffered severe psychological trauma, long-term mental health issues, or even death. MK-ULTRA remains a significant stain on the legacy of U.S. intelligence operations, illustrating the dangerous extremes that can result from unchecked power combined with Cold War paranoia.

EXPOSED:

Within the CIA, there were individuals who expressed discomfort or reservations about the ethical implications and efficacy of the MK-ULTRA experiments. As early as the mid-1960s, internal reviews raised questions about the project's validity and utility.

In 1973, fearing a leak and the potential for scandal, then-CIA Director Richard Helms ordered all MK-ULTRA files destroyed. While this move was intended to cover up the operation, it ironically raised suspicions when it later became apparent.

In 1974, *The New York Times* reported on the existence of the CIA's illegal domestic activities, leading to increased attention on the agency's operations. In 1975, due to a Freedom of Information Act (FOIA) request, a cache of documents related to MK-ULTRA was discovered. These were financial documents that had been spared from Helms' order of destruction because they were stored at a different location. They provided an accounting of the funds spent on the project and were a trail leading to the program's exposure.

The revelations from the FOIA discovery and the press led to a congressional investigation. In 1975, the Church Committee, led by Senator Frank Church, and the Rockefeller Commission, ordered by then-President Gerald Ford, began investigating the CIA's activities, including MK-ULTRA. Their findings were made public and brought the program to broader public awareness.

With the project's exposure, individuals who had been involved, either as researchers or subjects, began to come forward with their accounts, further solidifying the evidence of the program's existence and its controversial nature.

In the years following the exposure of MK-ULTRA, several individuals, or their families, who had been harmed by the experiments sought legal recourse, leading to court cases that further publicized details of the program.

The revelation of MK-ULTRA contributed to a more significant public awareness of the need for oversight and ethical standards in government research and operations, leading to reforms in how human research subjects are treated and protected.

FALLOUT FROM EXPOSURE:

The fallout from the revelation of MK-ULTRA was significant, both in terms of policy changes and its lasting legacy. Here's an outline of the repercussions and the long-term impact:

- The revelation that the U.S. government had conducted experiments on unwitting citizens, sometimes leading to significant harm or even death, generated substantial public shock and outrage. This was especially jarring given that the experiments included dosing individuals with LSD without their consent.

- Following the findings of the Church Committee and other investigations, Congress implemented reforms to ensure more robust oversight of the intelligence community.

- The revelations also played a role in the establishment of the Senate Select Committee on Intelligence in 1976, ensuring more consistent oversight of intelligence activities.

- The Belmont Report, published in 1979, laid out key ethical guidelines for human subjects research, including informed consent, beneficence, and justice.

- Lawsuits were filed by some victims of MK-ULTRA experiments. In some cases, the U.S. government reached settlements or paid reparations.

- MK-ULTRA has left a lasting mark on popular culture, becoming a frequent subject in books, movies, and television series. These references often focus on

themes of government conspiracy, mind
control, and the misuse of psychedelic drugs.

In summary, the legacy of MK-ULTRA is
multifaceted. While it brought about essential reforms
and heightened awareness of research ethics, it also left a
lasting scar on the public's trust in government and
became a cultural byword for government overreach and
conspiracy.

HOLLYWOOD INVOLVEMENT CONSPIRACY:

The "Hollywood connection" to MK-ULTRA often
refers to the idea that the entertainment industry has
either been influenced by the mind control objectives of
the program or has utilized its themes in various media.
There are two primary facets to this connection:

MK-ULTRA in Popular Culture:

- Films and TV Shows: Over the years,
numerous films and television shows have been inspired
by or have directly referenced MK-ULTRA. The
themes of mind control, government conspiracies, and
the covert use of drugs have proven to be compelling
subjects for narratives. Some films that touch on these
themes or are inspired by MK-ULTRA include "The
Manchurian Candidate" (both the original and its

remake), "Jacob's Ladder," "Conspiracy Theory," and the television series "Stranger Things," where the character Eleven's backstory draws inspiration from MK-ULTRA type experiments.

- **Documentaries**: There have also been documentary films and series exploring the real history of MK-ULTRA, often weaving in interviews with survivors, archival footage, and expert commentary.

Conspiracy Theories:

• There is a subset of conspiracy theories that suggest various celebrities have been subjected to MK-ULTRA or similar "mind control" programs. Proponents of these theories often interpret celebrities' behaviors, breakdowns, or even specific symbols in their music videos or photos as "evidence" of mind control.

• Such conspiracy theories often lack concrete evidence and can verge into sensationalism. It's also important to note that conflating personal struggles or mental health issues of celebrities with covert government programs can be both misleading and harmful. However, the idea has persisted in some conspiracy-minded communities and is often lumped in with broader conspiracy theories about the entertainment industry.

To clarify, while MK-ULTRA and its themes have been explored in Hollywood in terms of storytelling, there isn't concrete evidence linking the actual program to the entertainment industry in the way some conspiracy theories suggest. As with all conspiracy theories, it's crucial to approach such claims with skepticism and discernment and to differentiate between fictional depictions and real-world evidence.....but then again, it could be true as we all know.

* * *

CONSPIRACY THEORIES THAT WERE TRUE

Chapter Twenty-One

Madalyn Murray O'Hair

MADALYN MURRAY O'HAIR, often referred to as "The Most Hated Woman in America," was a prominent atheist activist who fought against religious influence in public institutions. Her disappearance in 1995, along with her son Jon Garth Murray and granddaughter Robin Murray O'Hair, remains one of the most perplexing and tragic mysteries of the 20th century.

* * *

Madalyn Murray O'Hair first came to national prominence in the early 1960s when she successfully challenged the mandatory prayer and Bible reading in public schools, leading to the landmark Supreme Court decision in Murray v. Curlett. Her outspoken atheism and combative personality made her a polarizing figure, earning her the ire of religious communities and the admiration of secularists.

By the mid-1990s, O'Hair had become a significant figure in American atheism, founding the organization American Atheists and continuing to campaign vigorously for the separation of church and state. However, her family life was tumultuous, marked by strained relationships and controversy.

In August 1995, Madalyn, Jon, and Robin suddenly disappeared from their home in Austin, Texas. Their disappearance initially went unnoticed due to the family's history of abruptly leaving town, often for extended periods, as part of their organizational activities or personal reasons. However, their prolonged absence soon raised alarms.

A peculiar aspect of their disappearance was the note left on the door of the American Atheists office, stating that the family had to attend to an emergency. This message was unusual and cryptic, leading to speculation about their whereabouts. The family had also withdrawn a substantial amount of money from the organization's accounts, further adding to the mystery.

The investigation into the disappearance was slow to start. Initially, the police showed little interest, partly due to the O'Hairs' controversial status and partly because of the misleading indications that the family had left voluntarily. It wasn't until months later that a serious inquiry began, driven largely by the persistent efforts of John MacCormack, a journalist with the San Antonio Express-News.

MacCormack's investigative work revealed several critical clues. One of the significant leads was the involvement of David Waters, a former office manager at American Atheists who had a criminal history and a tumultuous relationship with the O'Hairs. Waters had previously embezzled funds from the organization, leading to a contentious legal battle.

Throughout the investigation, numerous leads and eyewitness accounts surfaced, although many were conflicting and inconclusive. Some claimed to have seen the O'Hairs in various locations, but none of these sightings could be verified. The family seemed to have vanished without a trace, leaving no solid evidence of their fate.

One notable development was the discovery of a bank account in New Zealand in Jon Garth Murray's name, which contained a significant amount of money. This led to speculation that the family might have fled the country. However, further investigation revealed no activity on the account after the family's disappearance, casting doubt on this theory.

The breakthrough in the case came in 1999, when David Waters' involvement became more apparent. Waters, along with accomplices Gary Karr and Danny Fry, had kidnapped and murdered the O'Hairs. The motive was financial gain; Waters and his accomplices extorted a large sum of money from the family before brutally killing them.

Fry, one of the conspirators, was later found dismembered near Dallas, providing a critical link to the crime. His murder was believed to be an attempt by Waters to silence him. Waters and Karr were eventually convicted for their roles in the kidnapping and murders, but the exact details of the crime were pieced together through a combination of forensic evidence and confessions.

In 2001, the remains of Madalyn Murray O'Hair, Jon Garth Murray, and Robin Murray O'Hair were discovered on a remote Texas ranch. The bodies had been dismembered and buried, a gruesome end to a harrowing saga. The discovery brought some closure to the case, but many questions remained about the specifics of their final days and the full extent of Waters' conspiracy.

Several theories have emerged over the years regarding the disappearance and murder of the O'Hairs:

1. Financial Motive: The primary motive for the crime was financial. Waters and his accomplices sought to extort money from the O'Hairs, leveraging their control over the family's movements and resources.

2. Inside Job: There were suspicions that the crime was facilitated by someone within the organization. Waters' previous employment with American Atheists and his knowledge of their operations made him a prime suspect.

3. Personal Vendetta: Some have speculated that Waters harbored a personal grudge against Madalyn, stemming from his criminal past and their contentious

interactions. This vendetta may have fueled the brutal nature of the crime.

4. Conspiracy Theories* Various conspiracy theories have also circulated, including claims of involvement by other disgruntled employees or even external religious groups. However, these theories lack substantial evidence and are generally considered fringe speculations.

* * *

The disappearance and murder of Madalyn Murray O'Hair, Jon Garth Murray, and Robin Murray O'Hair is a chilling tale of betrayal, greed, and brutality. The case underscores the vulnerability of public figures, especially those who court controversy, and the lengths to which some will go to silence or exploit them.

Despite the resolution of the case with the convictions of Waters and Karr, the legacy of Madalyn Murray O'Hair remains complex.

Chapter Twenty-Two

Andrew Gosden

ANDREW GOSDEN, a 14-year-old boy from Doncaster, England, vanished on September 14, 2007. His disappearance has baffled investigators and left his family in a state of perpetual anguish. Despite extensive searches, media appeals, and numerous theories, Andrew's where-abouts remain unknown.

* * *

Andrew Gosden was born on July 10, 1993, in Doncaster, South Yorkshire. He was a bright student at McAuley Catholic High School, known for his intelligence and introverted nature. Andrew had a keen interest in video games and listening to music. He was also a member of the Young Gifted and Talented Programme, highlighting his academic prowess.

On the morning of September 14, 2007, Andrew left his home for what appeared to be a typical school day. However, instead of boarding the school bus, he returned home after his parents had left for work. Andrew changed out of his school uniform into casual clothes and withdrew £200 from his bank account. He then walked to Doncaster railway station and bought a one-way ticket to London, despite having the option to purchase a return ticket for just 50 pence more.

CCTV footage captured Andrew arriving at King's Cross Station in London at 11:20 AM. This was the last confirmed sighting of him. He did not take his PSP (a portable gaming device), charger, or any additional clothing, suggesting he did not plan to be away for long.

Andrew's parents, Kevin and Glenys Gosden, reported him missing when he did not return home that evening. The police initially treated his disappearance as a runaway case but soon realized it was more complex. They discovered that Andrew had not attended school and traced his movements to King's Cross Station.

Despite extensive media coverage and police appeals, no significant leads emerged. The investigation involved reviewing CCTV footage, interviewing witnesses, and conducting searches across London, but Andrew remained elusive.

Several unconfirmed sightings of Andrew were reported after his disappearance. A woman claimed to have seen a boy matching Andrew's description at a pizza restaurant in Covent Garden on the evening of his disappearance. Another witness reported seeing a boy resembling Andrew in the vicinity of Charing Cross Road around noon on the same day.

In the years following his disappearance, there have been sporadic reports of sightings, but none have been substantiated. These include alleged sightings at music festivals and various locations in London, but no concrete evidence has been found to confirm these reports.

Various theories have emerged regarding Andrew's disappearance, each adding to the mystery.

1. Runaway: One prevalent theory is that Andrew ran away to start a new life. However, his parents and friends insist that he showed no signs of unhappiness or desire to leave home permanently. Additionally, his actions, such as not taking his PSP or additional clothing, suggest he did not plan to be away for an extended period.

2. Foul Play: Another theory is that Andrew fell victim to foul play after arriving in London. The lack of CCTV footage after his arrival at King's Cross and no further financial activity on his bank account add weight to this possibility. London is a large city, and it is conceivable that he encountered someone with ill intentions.

3. Accident or Misadventure: Some speculate that Andrew may have suffered an accident or misadventure in London. This theory considers the possibility that he got lost, injured, or met with an accident that led to his death, with his body remaining undiscovered.

4. Mental Health Crisis: Although Andrew had no known mental health issues, some have suggested that he may have experienced a sudden mental health crisis, leading him to leave home and subsequently disappear.

5. Online Influences: With the rise of social media

and online communities, it has been suggested that Andrew may have been influenced or lured by someone he met online. This theory, however, remains speculative due to the lack of evidence showing his engagement in such activities.

Andrew's family has been relentless in their search for him. They have made numerous media appearances, set up a website and social media pages dedicated to finding Andrew, and distributed thousands of flyers. Despite these efforts, they have received few credible leads.

In 2018, on the 11th anniversary of his disappearance, the Gosden family made a renewed appeal for information, highlighting that Andrew would now be an adult. They emphasized the importance of any small piece of information that could lead to his whereabouts.

The investigation into Andrew's disappearance has seen the use of various technological tools. The police have utilized advancements in facial recognition software to analyze CCTV footage and age-progression technology to create images of what Andrew might look like today. These tools have been crucial in keeping the search alive and maintaining public interest in the case.

The emotional toll on the Gosden family has been immense. Kevin Gosden, Andrew's father, has spoken publicly about the pain and uncertainty of not knowing what happened to his son. The family has also been active in supporting other families of missing persons, using their experience to raise awareness about the challenges and emotional struggles faced by those left behind.

The disappearance of Andrew Gosden is a haunting mystery that has left a deep impact on his family, friends, and the wider community. Despite the passage of time, the search for Andrew continues, driven by the hope that he might still be found. The case remains open, with the police and Andrew's family urging anyone with information to come forward. Until then, the question of what happened to Andrew Gosden remains unanswered.

* * *

CONTINUE WITH
VANISHED: STRANGE & MYSTERIOUS
DISAPPEARANCES: VOLUME 3

Chapter Twenty-Three

The Sodder Children

ON THE NIGHT of December 24, 1945, a tragedy struck the Sodder family that would become one of the most enduring mysteries in American history. George and Jennie Sodder, Italian immigrants who had built a successful life in Fayetteville, West Virginia, were celebrating Christmas Eve with nine of their ten children.

As the family settled into bed, they had no idea that the events of the night would lead to the unexplained disappearance of five of their children: Maurice (14), Martha (12), Louis (9), Jennie (8), and Betty (5).

Around 12:30 a.m. on Christmas morning, Jennie Sodder was awakened by a phone call. The caller, a woman with an unfamiliar voice, asked for an unknown person. Jennie heard laughter and the clinking of glasses in the background. Assuming it was a prank call, Jennie hung up and noticed that the lights downstairs were still on and the front door was unlocked. She turned off the lights, locked the door, and went back to bed.

Shortly after, Jennie was awakened again, this time by the sound of something hitting the roof and then rolling off. She went back to sleep, only to wake up about thirty minutes later to the smell of smoke. She found that George's office, which also housed the telephone line and fuse box, was on fire. She woke George, and together they tried to rescue their children. George, Jennie, Marion, Sylvia, John, and George Jr. escaped the burning house, but the stairway to the attic, where the five youngest children slept, was engulfed in flames.

George Sodder's attempts to rescue the children were thwarted at every turn. The ladder, which he always kept propped against the house, was missing. He tried to use a barrel of water to douse the flames, but the water was frozen solid. George then attempted to drive his trucks, intending to use them to climb to the attic window, but neither truck would start, despite having been in perfect working order the previous day. Desperately, he broke a window, injuring his arm, but he could not get through the flames to reach the children.

The Fayetteville fire department, hampered by wartime shortages and relying on a "phone tree" system, did not respond until 8:00 a.m., seven hours after the fire had started. By that time, the Sodder home had been reduced to ashes. Fire Chief F.J. Morris and his men conducted a cursory search of the remains and declared that no bones or remains were found, suggesting that the fire had been hot enough to completely incinerate the bodies. However, this explanation was met with skepticism, as remnants of household appliances were found, and modern fire experts contend that bones should have remained.

From the beginning, George and Jennie Sodder were suspicious of the official explanation. They noted several unusual details and occurrences that led them to believe their children had been kidnapped. First, if the fire had been caused by faulty wiring, the power should have been out, yet the Christmas lights remained on during the early stages of the fire. Second, a witness later claimed to have seen a man at the fire scene taking a block and tackle used for removing car engines, possibly explaining why George's trucks failed to start.

Further adding to their suspicions, the ladder that was usually propped against the house was found at the bottom of an embankment, 75 feet away. A telephone repairman also informed the family that their phone line appeared to have been cut, not burned.

In the weeks and months following the fire, several eyewitnesses came forward with sightings of the missing Sodder children. A woman claimed to have seen the children in a car while the fire was still burning. Another woman, who ran a tourist stop between Fayetteville and Charleston, said she saw the children the morning after the fire. She served them breakfast and noted a car with Florida license plates at her establishment. Yet another witness, a woman at a Charleston hotel, reported seeing the children with two women and two men of Italian descent a week after the fire. She described the men as hostile and said they prevented her from speaking to the children.

Dissatisfied with the official investigation, George and Jennie Sodder hired private investigator C.C. Tinsley. Tinsley discovered that the insurance salesman who had threatened George was a member of the coroner's jury that ruled the fire accidental. Tinsley also learned from a local minister that Chief Morris had confided in him about finding a "heart" in the ashes, which he then buried. Upon exhumation, the "heart" was found to be a piece of beef liver, untouched by fire. This revelation led to further mistrust of the authorities' handling of the case.

In 1947, the Sodders appealed to the FBI for help. J. Edgar Hoover responded personally, stating that the FBI would assist if they received permission from local authorities. However, the Fayetteville police and fire departments declined the offer.

Over the years, the Sodders continued to search for their missing children. They distributed flyers, offered a $10,000 reward for information, and erected a billboard along Route 16 with photos of the missing children. The family received numerous tips and leads, some more credible than others. One such lead came in 1949 when the Sodders brought in a pathologist from Washington, D.C. to conduct a new search at the site. The pathologist found several small bone fragments, later identified as human vertebrae. However, it was determined that these bones likely came from the dirt George had used to bull-doze the site and were not related to the fire.

Many theories have been proposed to explain the disappearance of the Sodder children. Some speculate that the children were kidnapped by an Italian mafia, either in retaliation for George's outspoken criticism of

Mussolini or for other reasons. Others believe the children were taken and raised by another family. There are also theories suggesting that the children were victims of human trafficking.

Despite the numerous theories and ongoing investigations, the fate of the Sodder children remains a mystery. The surviving Sodder family members never gave up hope and continued to seek answers until their deaths. Jennie Sodder, in particular, wore black mourning clothes every day until her death in 1989, a testament to her unwavering belief that her children were still alive.

The disappearance of the Sodder children is a haunting and unresolved chapter in American history. The tragic events of Christmas Eve 1945 left a family shattered and a community bewildered. Despite extensive investigations, numerous leads, and the persistent efforts of George and Jennie Sodder, the mystery of what happened to Maurice, Martha, Louis, Jennie, and Betty Sodder remains unsolved. The case continues to intrigue and puzzle, a testament to the enduring power of a mystery that touches on the deepest fears and hopes of the human heart.

Chapter Twenty-Four

The Springfield Three

THE MYSTERIOUS DISAPPEARANCE of three women in Springfield, Missouri, known as "The Springfield Three," remains one of the most baffling unsolved cases in American history. The events unfolded in the early hours of June 7, 1992, when friends Stacy McCall, Suzanne "Suzie" Streeter, and Streeter's mother, Sherrill Levitt, vanished without a trace from Levitt's home. The case has confounded investigators and the public alike, leading to numerous theories and extensive investigations.

On the night of June 6, 1992, Stacy McCall and Suzie Streeter celebrated their recent graduation from Kickapoo High School. They attended multiple graduation parties and eventually decided to spend the night at Suzie's house, where her mother, Sherrill Levitt, lived. The last known sighting of the women was around 2 a.m. on June 7, when they were seen heading home.

The following morning, friends Janelle Kirby and Mike Henson visited the house after McCall and Streeter failed to show up for a planned trip to a water park. Upon arrival, they found the front door unlocked and entered, noticing all three women's cars parked outside. Inside, the house appeared undisturbed, except for a shattered porch light. They found Levitt and Streeter's dog, Cinnamon, visibly agitated. Kirby answered a strange and disturbing phone call filled with sexual innuendos, which she hung up on, only to receive another similar call shortly after.

Hours later, McCall's mother, Janis, arrived at the house, deeply concerned after failing to reach her daughter by phone. She found the women's purses, including Levitt's purse with over $800 in cash, inside the house. Additionally, McCall's clothing from the previous night was neatly folded, and there were no signs of a struggle. The television was left on, showing static, suggesting it had been on all night.

The Springfield Police Department was contacted, and they arrived to find a potential crime scene that had already been compromised by numerous visitors. Despite this, they noted that there were no signs of forced entry or a violent struggle. Investigators considered the possibility that the women had been abducted by someone they knew and trusted.

Early theories suggested that Sherrill Levitt might have been the primary target due to her background as a single mother and a cosmetologist who might have had contentious relationships with clients. Another theory proposed that Suzie Streeter, who was known to associate with a troubled crowd, might have been the intended victim. However, a random act of violence could not be ruled out, given the lack of clear evidence pointing to a specific suspect.

Several suspects emerged over the years, with two standing out prominently:

1. Dustin Recla: A former boyfriend of Suzie Streeter, Recla had a criminal history, including a charge for vandalizing a mausoleum. Streeter had given a statement to the police about Recla's involvement in the

crime, and it was believed she might testify against him in court. However, no concrete evidence linked Recla to the disappearances.

2. Robert Craig Cox: A convicted kidnapper and murderer, Cox was living in Springfield at the time of the disappearances. He claimed to know what happened to the women, suggesting they had been murdered and their bodies would never be found. However, Cox's statements were inconsistent, and investigators were unsure whether he was genuinely involved or seeking attention.

Additionally, a tip in 2007 led to a search of the Cox Hospital parking garage, where ground-penetrating radar detected anomalies resembling graves. Despite this, authorities decided not to excavate, citing the lack of credible evidence and the high cost of such an operation.

Various theories have been proposed over the years, ranging from plausible to far-fetched:

1. Abduction by a Known Person: Given the lack of forced entry and signs of struggle, it's possible the women were abducted by someone they knew and trusted. This theory aligns with the idea that a single

perpetrator with a gun could have subdued them without a struggle.

2. Random Act of Violence: Another theory suggests that a random predator might have targeted the women. This aligns with the notion of a sexual sadist driving around Springfield and following the women home from their graduation parties.

3. Burial in a Remote Location: Some believe the women were taken to a remote location and buried. The Mark Twain National Forest and a hog farm in Webster County have been suggested as potential sites, but searches yielded no results.

4. Involvement of Multiple Perpetrators: Although an FBI profiler suggested a single perpetrator, some believe multiple individuals might have been involved, possibly from Suzie Streeter's social circle.

Despite numerous tips and extensive media coverage, the case remains unsolved. In 1997, Levitt and Streeter were declared legally dead, though their case files remain open and classified as missing persons. Over 5,000 tips have been received, but none have led to a breakthrough.

The case has been featured in various media, including

television shows like "48 Hours" and "America's Most Wanted," as well as true crime podcasts. These platforms have kept public interest alive and occasionally generated new leads, though none have conclusively solved the mystery.

The disappearance of The Springfield Three continues to haunt the community and investigators alike. Despite the passage of over three decades, the case remains an enigma, with no definitive answers as to what happened to Stacy McCall, Suzie Streeter, and Sherrill Levitt. Theories abound, and suspects have come and gone, but the truth remains elusive. As the search for answers continues, the hope persists that someday, the mystery will be solved, bringing closure to the families and the community.

Chapter Twenty-Five

Tara Calico

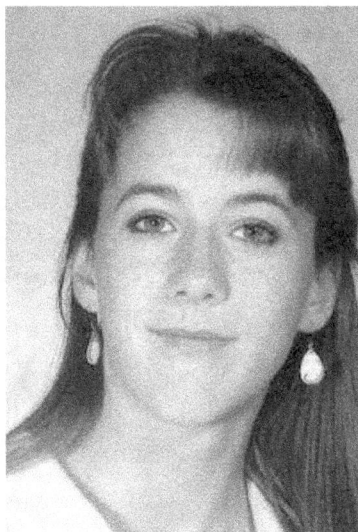

THE DISAPPEARANCE of Tara Calico on September 20, 1988, remains one of the most perplexing and unsettling mysteries in American history. Tara, a 19-year-old college student, vanished without a trace during a routine bike ride along Highway 47 in Valencia County, New Mexico. Despite exhaustive searches, numerous investigations, and several theories, her fate remains unknown. This chapter delves into the details of her disappearance, the investigation, and the enduring mystery surrounding the case.

Tara Calico left her home around 9:30 a.m. on her mother's pink Huffy bike. She had planned to be back by noon to play tennis with her boyfriend and later attend a class at the University of New Mexico at Valencia. Tara had a routine route along Highway 47, which she rode almost daily. Before leaving, she jokingly told her mother, Patty Doel, to come look for her if she wasn't back by noon.

When Tara did not return by noon, Patty began to worry. She drove along Tara's usual route but found no sign of her daughter. She contacted the authorities immediately. The next day, Patty discovered a Boston cassette tape and part of Tara's Sony Walkman near the route, suggesting a possible struggle. Witnesses reported seeing a light-colored pickup truck with a camper shell following Tara that morning. Despite these clues, the initial search yielded no significant evidence of Tara's whereabouts.

The investigation into Tara's disappearance was

extensive. Authorities interviewed several witnesses who had seen the pickup truck. Some reported that the truck appeared to be following Tara closely. The truck, described as a 1953 Ford, became a key piece of evidence, but it was never located.

Nine months after Tara vanished, a Polaroid photograph was found in a convenience store parking lot in Port St. Joe, Florida. The photograph depicted a young woman and a boy, both bound and gagged. The girl in the photo bore a striking resemblance to Tara, and the book visible in the picture, "My Sweet Audrina" by V.C. Andrews, was one of Tara's favorite books. Despite the FBI's involvement, the identities of the individuals in the photograph could not be conclusively confirmed.

In the years following, two other photographs surfaced, depicting a girl resembling Tara in distressing situations. These images were found in different locations and on film that was produced after Tara's disappearance. Despite these leads, none of the photos could be definitively linked to Tara.

Over the years, several theories have emerged regarding Tara's fate. One prominent theory, proposed by Valencia County Sheriff Rene Rivera in 2008, suggested that two local teenage boys accidentally hit Tara with their truck, panicked, and then killed her to cover up the accident. Rivera claimed to know the identities of the boys and their accomplices but stated that without Tara's body, he could not make an arrest. This theory has been met with skepticism and controversy, as Rivera did not disclose the evidence supporting his claims.

Another theory involves a series of threatening notes that were reportedly left on Tara's car in the months leading up to her disappearance. Some investigators believe that Tara may have been targeted by someone who knew her and had malicious intent. Despite these theories, no arrests have been made, and the case remains open.

In October 2019, the FBI announced a $20,000 reward for information leading to Tara's identification or the arrest of those responsible for her disappearance. In September 2021, the Valencia County Sheriff's Office and the New Mexico State Police issued a statement about a new lead in the case, involving a sealed warrant for an unknown private residence. In June 2023, Sheriff Denise Vigil announced a breakthrough in the case, stating that there was sufficient evidence to submit the investigation to the district attorney for review. However, details about the persons of interest remain sealed by the court.

The disappearance of Tara Calico continues to haunt her family, friends, and the community. Despite numerous leads, extensive investigations, and widespread media attention, her fate remains unknown. The case exemplifies the challenges and complexities of missing person investigations and the enduring pain of unresolved disappearances. As new information comes to light, there remains hope that one day the mystery of what happened to Tara Calico will be solved.

Chapter Twenty-Six

Richey Edwards

RICHARD JAMES EDWARDS, affectionately known as Richey, was born on December 22, 1967, in Blackwood, Wales. As the lyricist and rhythm guitarist for the Welsh alternative rock band Manic Street Preachers, Edwards became an iconic figure in the early 1990s. His profound and often dark lyrics resonated deeply with fans, while his enigmatic personality and troubled soul made him a subject of fascination and concern.

Edwards was a man of contradictions. He was charismatic yet deeply insecure, intellectual yet emotionally fragile. His lyrics were rich with literary references and existential musings, reflecting his admiration for writers like Sylvia Plath and Arthur Rimbaud. Despite his limited musical proficiency, Edwards' contribution to the band's identity was immeasurable, often being the intellectual and creative force behind their distinctive style.

In the weeks leading up to his disappearance, Edwards' behavior became increasingly erratic. He was known to struggle with severe depression, anorexia, and a history of self-harm. In early 1995, he entered a rehabilitation clinic, but his condition seemed to deteriorate further upon his release.

In January 1995, Edwards withdrew significant amounts of cash from his bank account, totaling £2,800. This action was puzzling and left his friends and family speculating about his intentions. On February 1, 1995, the day he was supposed to fly to the United States with bandmate James Dean Bradfield for a promotional tour, Edwards checked out of the Embassy Hotel in London early in the morning. He took his wallet, car keys, Prozac, and passport but left behind a packed suitcase and other personal belongings.

The Disappearance: A Timeline of Events:

- February 1, 1995: After checking out of the hotel, Edwards drove to his apartment in Cardiff. He left behind his passport and some Prozac, indicating he might have planned to return. This was the last confirmed sighting of him.
- February 7, 1995: A taxi driver from Newport claimed to have picked up Edwards and driven him around the valleys, including his hometown of Blackwood. The driver described Edwards as speaking in a Cockney accent that occasionally slipped into a Welsh one. The passenger asked to be taken to various locations before finally getting out at the Severn View service station near Aust, Gloucestershire.

- February 14, 1995: Edwards' Vauxhall
  Cavalier received a parking ticket at the
  Severn View service station. The vehicle
  was reported as abandoned on February 17.
  Inside the car, police found evidence
  suggesting it had been lived in, including
  photographs Edwards had taken of his
  family in the days prior. The proximity of
  the car to the Severn Bridge, a known suicide
  site, led many to speculate that Edwards had
  taken his own life by jumping from the
  bridge.

The South Wales Police launched an extensive investigation following Edwards' disappearance. Initial efforts included a thorough search of the Severn Bridge area, using sonar equipment to scan the river. However, no trace of Edwards was found. Interviews with friends, family, and potential witnesses were conducted, but they yielded little concrete information.

One significant lead came from the aforementioned taxi driver, who provided a detailed account of his interactions with Edwards on February 7. According to the driver, Edwards was agitated and restless during the journey, often changing his mind about destinations and asking peculiar questions.

Despite this promising lead, it did not result in any definitive conclusions.

Theories and Speculations: What Happened to Richey Edwards?

Numerous theories have emerged over the years regarding Edwards' disappearance. Each theory has its proponents and detractors, reflecting the enigmatic nature of the case.

1. Suicide: The most widely accepted theory is that Edwards committed suicide by jumping from the Severn Bridge. His mental health struggles and the location of his abandoned car support this theory. However, the absence of a body and the lack of definitive evidence leave room for doubt.

2. Voluntary Disappearance: Another theory posits that Edwards staged his own disappearance to escape the pressures of fame and his personal demons. The substantial cash withdrawals and unconfirmed sightings of him in various locations, including Goa and the Canary Islands, lend some credence to this idea. However, the logistics and the apparent lack of preparation (e.g., leaving his passport behind) complicate this theory.

3. Foul Play: While less commonly believed, some speculate that Edwards may have been a victim of foul play. This theory suggests he was abducted or murdered, but there is scant evidence to support such a scenario. The investigation has not uncovered any leads pointing to foul play.

Richey Edwards' life was marked by his profound intellect, artistic brilliance, and deep personal struggles. Born into a mining family in Blackwood, he excelled academically and developed a passion for literature and music. He formed a close bond with Nicky Wire, who would become his collaborator in the Manic Street Preachers.

Edwards' contributions to the band were instrumental in their rise to fame. His lyrics, often dark and introspective, resonated with a generation of fans. Songs like "4st 7lb," which candidly addressed his battle with anorexia, and "Yes," with its raw depiction of prostitution and exploitation, showcased his ability to channel personal pain into powerful art.

Despite the band's success, Edwards struggled to cope with the demands of fame. His mental health issues were exacerbated by the pressures of the music industry, leading to several stints in rehabilitation. His disappearance in 1995 marked the tragic culmination of years of inner turmoil.

The disappearance of Richey Edwards had a profound impact on those who knew him and the legions of fans who admired him. His family, particularly his sister Rachel, has been vocal about the emotional toll of his absence. For years, they held out hope that Edwards might still be alive, but in 2008, he was officially declared presumed dead.

Bandmates Nicky Wire, James Dean Bradfield, and Sean Moore have often spoken about the loss of their friend and collaborator. Edwards' absence left a void in the band, both personally and creatively. They continued to honor his legacy in their music, with several albums featuring lyrics he had written before his disappearance.

Richey Edwards' influence extends beyond his music. He has become a cultural icon, symbolizing the tortured artist who struggles with inner demons while creating profound art. His lyrics, interviews, and public persona continue to be studied and admired by fans and scholars alike.

Books, documentaries, and articles have been dedicated to exploring his life and the mystery of his disappearance. Edwards' story serves as a cautionary tale about the pressures of fame and the importance of mental health support for artists.

Nearly three decades after his disappearance, Richey Edwards remains an enduring mystery in the world of rock music. His life and work continue to resonate with those who find solace and inspiration in his art. Whether he chose to vanish or met a tragic end, Edwards' legacy lives on through his music and the lasting impact he made on fans and fellow musicians.

Chapter Twenty-Seven

Bison Dele

BISON DELE, born Brian Carson Williams, was a former NBA player known for his athletic prowess and adventurous spirit. His life took a mysterious turn when he disappeared in 2002, along with his girlfriend Serena Karlan and the boat's skipper, Bertrand Saldo, while sailing in the South Pacific. This chapter delves into the details of their disappearance, the ensuing investigation, and the theories that surround this baffling case.

Bison played for several teams, including the Orlando Magic, Denver Nuggets, LA Clippers, Chicago Bulls, and Detroit Pistons. Standing at 6 foot 10 inches tall, he was an imposing force on the court. In 1998, he changed his name to honor his Native American and African American heritage. Dele retired from professional basketball in 1999 at the peak of his career, choosing to explore a life of adventure. He traveled extensively, learned to sail, and purchased a catamaran named "Hakuna Matata".

Dele's retirement was abrupt and surprising to many. At the time, he was one of the highest-paid players on the Detroit Pistons with a $36 million contract. Despite this financial security and professional success, Dele was known for his free-spirited nature. He earned a pilot's license, biked across the United States, and traveled to various exotic locations including Lebanon, the Mediterranean, and the Australian outback.

Serena Karlan, Dele's girlfriend, was described as a beautiful and kind-hearted woman from Berkeley, California. She had a transient career, working in various jobs until she met Dele. Their relationship blossomed quickly, and Serena joined Dele in his adventures. Bertrand Saldo, the skipper of the Hakuna Matata, was an experienced sailor responsible for navigating the boat.

In July 2002, Dele, Karlan, and Saldo set sail from Tahiti on the Hakuna Matata. Dele's estranged brother, Miles Dabord (born Kevin Williams), joined them shortly before their departure. The group planned to sail to Hawaii, with stops along the way. However, the trip was marred by tension between the brothers. Dabord, who was financially struggling, had a history of conflicts with Dele.

On July 6, 2002, the voyage began. For the first couple of days, everything seemed to be going well. Dele and Karlan maintained regular contact with their families and banks, making three satellite phone calls during this period. The last call was made by Karlan on July 8, 2002, to Dele's business manager, Kevin Porter, reporting that everything was fine and everyone was happy.

After the last phone call, all communication from the Hakuna Matata ceased. When days passed without any contact, the families of Dele and Karlan grew increasingly concerned. They reported the disappearance to the authorities, prompting a large-scale search effort. The U.S. Coast Guard issued a telex distress bulletin to all ships within a 1,000-mile radius of Tahiti, but there was no sign of the catamaran or its occupants.

On July 20, 2002, Miles Dabord sailed the Hakuna Matata back into Tahiti alone. The boat had been repainted and renamed "Aria Bella," with its original nameplate removed. Dabord's solitary return and the altered state of the boat immediately raised suspicions.

The investigation into the disappearance of Bison Dele, Serena Karlan, and Bertrand Saldo was complex and involved multiple agencies, including the FBI and French authorities. The initial findings were troubling. It was discovered that Dabord had been using Dele's identity to conduct financial transactions. On September 5, 2002, Dabord attempted to purchase gold coins worth $152,000 using Dele's passport and checkbook. This led to his detention in Phoenix, Arizona.

During interrogation, Dabord claimed he was acting on behalf of Dele, who was supposedly alive but in trouble. However, there was no way to verify this claim as Dele, Karlan, and Saldo were still missing. The police had to release Dabord due to insufficient evidence.

Eyewitnesses reported seeing a catamaran resembling the Hakuna Matata being brought into Phaeton Bay, Tahiti, by a man matching Dabord's description. The boat had noticeable changes, including patched bullet holes and its new name, "Aria Bella." These alterations added to the suspicions surrounding Dabord's involvement.

Erica Weise, Dabord's girlfriend, provided a crucial piece of the puzzle. She told police that Dabord had confessed to her about the events on the boat. According to her, Dabord said that Karlan was accidentally killed during a fight between the brothers. In a panic, Dele killed Saldo when the skipper attempted to report Karlan's death. Dabord then claimed he shot Dele in self-defense and disposed of the bodies by throwing them overboard, weighted down with objects to ensure they wouldn't resurface.

After his release from police custody, Dabord fled to Mexico. On September 14, 2002, he was found unconscious on a beach in Tijuana, having overdosed on insulin. He was brought back to the United States but died in a California hospital on September 27, 2002. With his death, any chance of discovering the full truth of what happened on the Hakuna Matata vanished.

The prevailing theory, supported by the FBI and French authorities, is that Miles Dabord murdered Dele, Karlan, and Saldo. The evidence included forged documents, suspicious financial transactions, and the altered state of the catamaran. However, without the bodies or concrete forensic evidence, this theory remains speculative.

Another theory suggests that the motive behind the murders was greed and jealousy. Dabord, who was financially destitute, may have seen an opportunity to benefit from his brother's wealth. The estranged relationship between the brothers and Dabord's previous financial troubles lend credence to this motive.

Some have speculated that the murders were premeditated. The purchase of weights by Dabord before the voyage suggests a level of planning. These weights were likely used to ensure the bodies would sink and not be discovered. The alterations to the boat, including the removal of its nameplate and the patched bullet holes, further indicate a cover-up.

The disappearance of Bison Dele, Serena Karlan, and Bertrand Saldo had a profound impact on their families and friends. Dele's family struggled with the loss of both sons, as Dabord's death closed the door on any chance of finding answers. Serena Karlan's family held a memorial service in Berkeley, California, to honor her memory. The case attracted significant media attention, drawing public interest and speculation.

Bison Dele's legacy as a talented athlete and adventurer lives on, even as the details of his final days remain shrouded in mystery. His decision to leave a lucrative

NBA career for a life of exploration and adventure is both inspiring and tragic. The case continues to intrigue and baffle investigators and the public alike, serving as a poignant reminder of the uncertainties that can lurk behind even the most adventurous and seemingly fulfilling lives.

In the wake of this tragedy, memorial services were held for Dele, Karlan, and Dabord. Dele's legacy as a talented athlete and adventurer lives on, even as the details of his final days remain shrouded in mystery. The case of Bison Dele stands as a testament to the complexities of human relationships and the dark turns that life can sometimes take.

The disappearance of Bison Dele, Serena Karlan, and Bertrand Saldo remains one of the most perplexing mysteries of the past century. The lack of concrete evidence and the death of the primary suspect, Miles Dabord, have left many questions unanswered. The case continues to intrigue and baffle investigators and the public alike, serving as a poignant reminder of the uncertainties that can lurk behind even the most adventurous and seemingly fulfilling lives.

Chapter Twenty-Eight

Asha Degree

ASHA JAQUILLA DEGREE, a nine-year-old girl from Shelby, North Carolina, disappeared on Valentine's Day, 2000. The circumstances of her disappearance are both perplexing and heart-wrenching. Asha lived with her parents, Harold and Iquilla Degree, and her older brother, O'Bryant. The family resided in a small apartment complex, leading a life that seemed typical and stable.

On the night of February 13, 2000, Asha went to bed after a routine evening. She shared a room with her brother, and their father checked on them around 2:30 AM. Both children were sound asleep. However, by 6:30 AM, Asha was gone. Her bed was empty, and the front door of the house was locked from the inside, with no signs of forced entry.

Several witnesses reported seeing Asha walking along Highway 18 in the early hours of February 14. Around 4:00 AM, a truck driver and a motorist saw her walking south, away from her home. The weather was inclement, with heavy rain and strong winds, making the sight of a young girl alone on the highway even more unusual. One motorist even turned around, concerned for her safety, but reported that Asha ran into the woods when he approached her.

Asha's family contacted the police as soon as they discovered her absence. The initial search focused on the area around her home and along the highway where she was last seen. Volunteers, law enforcement officers, and search dogs combed the area, but found no immediate traces of Asha.

On February 15, 2000, searchers found candy wrappers, a pencil, a green marker, and a yellow hairbow in a shed near the highway where Asha was last seen. These items were identified as belonging to Asha, providing the first concrete evidence of her movements. However, despite an extensive search that included over 9,000 man-hours and covered a two-to-three-mile radius, no further clues were discovered.

As the days turned into weeks, the investigation into Asha's disappearance intensified. The FBI and North Carolina's State Bureau of Investigation (SBI) became involved. Given Asha's young age and the circumstances of her disappearance, various theories emerged.

1. Runaway Theory: Some investigators initially considered the possibility that Asha had run away. This theory was based on the items she took with her, which suggested some degree of planning. However, experts and those close to Asha argued against this theory, noting that it was unusual for a child so young, with no apparent issues at home or school, to run away. Additionally, most runaway cases involve children aged 12 and older.

2. Abduction: Another prevailing theory was that Asha might have been abducted. The fact that she disappeared without a trace and was seen running into the woods suggested she might have encountered

someone with ill intentions. However, there was no direct evidence of an abduction, and the lack of immediate suspects made this theory difficult to prove.

3. Accidental Death and Concealment: Some speculated that Asha might have met with an accident and that someone, fearing repercussions, might have concealed her body. This theory, too, lacked concrete evidence but remained a possibility due to the circumstances surrounding her disappearance.

The case saw sporadic developments over the years. In August 2001, a significant breakthrough occurred when Asha's bookbag was discovered buried along Highway 18 in Burke County, about 26 miles north of Shelby. The bookbag contained several items, including a Dr. Seuss book and a New Kids on the Block T-shirt, neither of which belonged to Asha before her disappearance. This discovery renewed hope in the investigation but also raised further questions.

In 2017, the FBI's Child Abduction Rapid Deployment (CARD) Team was brought in to re-evaluate the case. This specialized team meticulously reviewed all evidence, hoping to identify new leads or eliminate false ones. Despite their efforts, no new substantial evidence was found. However, their involvement underscored the ongoing commitment to solving Asha's case.

The CARD Team's deployment also highlighted the advancements in investigative techniques since Asha's disappearance. Enhanced DNA technology and a better understanding of child abductions have provided new avenues for investigation. The hope remains that these advancements might eventually lead to a breakthrough.

The case has continued to receive significant media attention over the years. The Degree family has made numerous public appeals, appearing on national television shows like "The Montel Williams Show," "America's Most Wanted," and "The Oprah Winfrey Show." These appearances aimed to keep Asha's story alive in the public consciousness and encourage anyone with information to come forward.

Local efforts have also been persistent. Billboards featuring Asha's image and details about her disappearance have been erected, and her story is regularly featured in local news outlets. The community's involvement and the media's ongoing coverage have been crucial in keeping the search for Asha active.

Over the years, numerous theories and speculations have surfaced, but none have led to a definitive answer. Some believe that Asha might have been lured away by someone she knew, while others think she might have been the victim of a random abduction. The discovery of her bookbag, with unfamiliar items, suggests she might have come into contact with someone who played a role in her disappearance.

Another intriguing lead came in 2016 when an inmate claimed to know what happened to Asha. He alleged that she had been killed and provided specific information that led to a search in the Lawndale area. However, this search yielded no new evidence, and the inmate's claims remain unverified.

The disappearance of Asha Degree remains one of the most baffling and heartbreaking cases in recent history. Despite extensive investigations, numerous searches, and the involvement of various law enforcement agencies, Asha's whereabouts and the circumstances of her disappearance remain unknown.

For Asha's family and the community of Shelby, the search for answers continues. The hope is that with advancements in technology and persistent public interest, someone will come forward with the crucial piece of information needed to solve this case.

Asha's story is a poignant reminder of the enduring impact of unresolved disappearances and the relentless pursuit of justice for missing children. As technology advances and new leads are pursued, there remains hope that one day, Asha Degree will be found, and the questions that have haunted her family and community for over two decades will finally be answered.

Chapter Twenty-Nine

Lars Mittank

THE CASE of Lars Mittank is one of the most enigmatic and widely discussed missing person cases in recent history. This chapter explores the intricate details of Lars's disappearance, including the events leading up to it, the investigation that followed, eyewitness accounts, and the various theories that have emerged over the years.

Lars Joachim Mittank was born on February 9, 1986, in Berlin, Germany. Described as a diligent and friendly individual, Lars worked as an engineer and led a stable life. In June 2014, he decided to take a holiday to Varna, Bulgaria, with a group of his close friends. The trip was intended to be a time for relaxation and fun, enjoying the sunny beaches and lively nightlife of the coastal city.

On the night of July 6, 2014, during the last days of their holiday, Lars and his friends visited a bar in Varna. A dispute broke out between Lars and other German tourists over football team loyalties. Although the argument appeared to settle down initially, later that night, Lars was attacked by locals, allegedly hired by the tourists he had quarreled with earlier. This attack left him with a perforated eardrum and an injured jaw.

The following day, Lars sought medical attention for his injuries. The doctor diagnosed him with a ruptured eardrum and advised against flying due to the potential danger posed by changes in air pressure. Instead, Lars was prescribed the antibiotic Cefprozil to prevent infection and was advised to rest for a few days before flying home. Despite his friends' offers to stay with him, Lars insisted that they return home as planned. He then moved to the budget-friendly Hotel Color, close to the airport, intending to fly back to Germany once he felt better.

After his friends left, Lars's behavior took a disturbing turn. He exhibited signs of extreme paranoia and anxiety, calling his mother, Sandra Mittank, several times and whispering that he was being followed and his life was in danger. Surveillance footage from the Hotel Color captured him pacing the halls, peering out of windows, and hiding in the elevator. At around 1:00 a.m., he was seen leaving the hotel but returned an hour later. His mother recalled that during one of their phone conversations, Lars asked her to cancel his credit cards because he believed they had been compromised.

On the morning of July 8, Lars decided to go to Varna Airport, hoping to catch a flight back to Germany. He took a taxi to the airport and informed his mother that he had arrived. Lars then went to see Dr. Kosta Kostov, the airport physician, to get clearance to fly. Dr. Kostov described Lars as extremely nervous and agitated. During their consultation, a construction worker entered the office, which seemed to trigger a panic attack in Lars. He shouted, "I don't want to die here. I have to get out of here," before fleeing the office, leaving behind all his belongings, including his wallet, phone, and passport.

CCTV footage captured Lars running through the airport terminal, exiting the building, climbing a fence, and disappearing into a nearby meadow and sunflower field located beside the Bulgarian national highway A2. This was the last confirmed sighting of Lars Mittank.

The initial investigation into Lars's disappearance involved extensive searches by Bulgarian authorities. They combed the area surrounding the airport, including the meadow and the nearby forest, but found no trace of him. His mother, Sandra, who had been in constant communication with Lars before his disappearance, traveled to Bulgaria to aid in the search efforts. She also hired a private investigator, Andreas Gütig, who checked hospitals, shelters, and morgues for any sign of Lars. Despite these efforts, no substantial leads were found.

Over the years, there have been multiple reported sightings of Lars in various countries. In 2015, a man resembling Lars was seen in Porto Velho, Brazil, but this lead did not pan out. Another potential sighting occurred in 2019 when a German truck driver claimed to have given a ride to a hitchhiker who looked like an older version of Lars. These sightings have kept hope alive but have not provided any concrete answers.

Several theories have been proposed to explain Lars Mittank's disappearance, each with its own set of supporting arguments and counterpoints.

1. Psychotic Episode: One of the leading theories is that Lars experienced a psychotic episode, possibly triggered by the antibiotic Cefprozil. This medication has known side effects, including hallucinations and paranoia. However, Dr. Kostov noted that Lars had not filled his prescription, casting doubt on this theory. Another possibility is that Lars suffered from an undiagnosed mental illness, such as schizophrenia, which manifested suddenly under the stress of his injuries and being alone in a foreign country.

2. Criminal Involvement: Some speculate that Lars might have been involved in criminal activities, possibly drug trafficking, and was trying to escape from dangerous associates. This theory could explain his extreme paranoia and erratic behavior. However, there is little evidence to support this, and Lars's family and friends have dismissed the idea, citing his responsible and law-abiding nature.

3. Foul Play: Given Lars's claims that he was being followed and the violent attack he experienced,

some believe that he might have been targeted by criminals. This theory suggests that he could have been abducted or killed after fleeing the airport. The fact that no body has been found supports the possibility that he was taken far from the search area.

4. Voluntary Disappearance: Another theory posits that Lars voluntarily disappeared to start a new life. This idea seems unlikely given his close relationship with his family and the fact that he left all his belongings behind. Moreover, Lars was in constant contact with his mother and friends, showing no signs of wanting to abandon his life.

5. Accidental Death: Some believe that Lars might have died accidentally after fleeing the airport. The area surrounding the airport includes dense forests and rugged terrain, which could be dangerous for someone in a disoriented state. However, despite extensive searches, no evidence of an accident has been found.

Several eyewitness accounts have surfaced over the years, each adding a layer of mystery to the case. Hotel staff at the Hotel Color reported that Lars appeared extremely agitated during his stay. They noted his strange behavior, including his frequent pacing and constant checking of windows. The taxi driver who took him to the airport described him as anxious and in a hurry, although there were no signs of physical harm or immediate danger.

Dr. Kosta Kostov, the airport physician, provided a crucial account of Lars's behavior at the airport. He described Lars as highly nervous and erratic, particularly after a construction worker entered the office. This interaction seemed to trigger an intense fear response in Lars, leading him to flee in a state of panic. Dr. Kostov's testimony highlighted the severity of Lars's mental state at the time of his disappearance.

The search efforts for Lars Mittank were extensive and involved multiple parties. Bulgarian authorities conducted ground and aerial searches in the area surrounding the airport. They utilized drones, search dogs, and volunteers to comb through the dense forest and rugged terrain. Despite these efforts, no trace of Lars was found.

Sandra Mittank, Lars's mother, was relentless in her search for her son. She traveled to Bulgaria multiple times, coordinating with local authorities and hiring private investigators to aid in the search. Sandra also appealed to the public for information, distributing flyers and leveraging social media to raise awareness about Lars's disappearance. Her efforts brought international attention to the case, but unfortunately, they did not yield any concrete leads.

Dr. Todd Grande, a certified mental health counselor, has analyzed Lars Mittank's case in detail. He proposed that Lars might have experienced "first break psychosis" or the onset of a severe mental illness such as schizophrenia. According to Dr. Grande, the sudden and extreme nature of Lars's paranoia and erratic behavior could be indicative of a psychotic episode. This theory aligns with the reports of Lars's behavior at the hotel and the airport, where he exhibited signs of intense fear and confusion.

Lars Mittank's case gained significant attention on social media, particularly on platforms like YouTube, where the CCTV footage of his disappearance has been viewed millions of times. This widespread exposure has led to numerous tips and alleged sightings, though none have been substantiated. Online sleuths and amateur investigators continue to discuss and analyze the case, contributing to the ongoing search for answers.

The disappearance of Lars Mittank remains one of the most baffling and unresolved mysteries of recent times. Despite extensive investigations, numerous theories, and widespread media attention, Lars's fate is still unknown. His family continues to hope for his return, clinging to the belief that he might be out there somewhere, possibly suffering from amnesia or another condition that prevents him from returning home.

The case of Lars Mittank is one of the most enigmatic and widely discussed missing person cases in recent history. This chapter explores the intricate details of Lars's disappearance, including the events leading up to it, the investigation that followed, eyewitness accounts, and the various theories that have emerged over the years.

Chapter Thirty

The Beaumont Children

THE DISAPPEARANCE of the Beaumont children on January 26, 1966, is one of Australia's most enduring and tragic mysteries. Jane, aged 9, Arnna, aged 7, and Grant, aged 4, vanished from Glenelg Beach in Adelaide, sparking one of the largest searches in the nation's history and an investigation that has persisted for over five decades.

It was a scorching summer day when Nancy Beaumont sent her three children to Glenelg Beach, a short bus ride from their home in Somerton Park. The children had made this trip several times before and were expected to return by 2:00 PM. When they failed to come home, Nancy became worried. By 5:00 PM, after searching in vain and contacting her husband Jim, they reported the children missing to the police.

The initial investigation mobilized a massive land, sea, and air search involving police, the army, navy, air force, and thousands of volunteers. The search extended from Glenelg Beach to surrounding areas, including homes, businesses, and parks. Despite these efforts, no trace of the children was found.

Several eyewitnesses reported seeing the Beaumont children with a tall, blond, sun-tanned man on the day of their disappearance. This man, described as being in his 30s and wearing blue swim trunks, was seen playing with the children and later helping them dress. A local bakery employee also recalled the children purchasing pastries with a £1 note, far more than the pocket money their mother had given them. This led investigators to believe that the children had been given the money by someone else, presumably the man seen with them.

Another significant sighting was reported by a postman who knew the children and saw them around 3:00 PM walking happily away from the beach along Jetty Road, seemingly unconcerned about their late return.

Over the years, several suspects have been considered, but none have been definitively linked to the crime.

1. Harry Phipps: A wealthy local businessman who operated the Castalloy factory near the beach. Phipps matched the description of the man seen with the children. His son later claimed to have seen the children in their yard on the day they disappeared. In 2013 and 2018, police excavated parts of Phipps' factory based on witness accounts of a hole being dug shortly after the disappearance, but found nothing.

2. Bevan Spencer von Einem: A convicted child killer who allegedly boasted about abducting three children from a beach. Despite his confessions, no evidence was found to link him directly to the Beaumont case.

3. Arthur Stanley Brown: Another suspect linked to the disappearance due to his conviction in other child abduction cases. He too, however, could not be definitively connected to the Beaumonts.

Desperate for answers, the Beaumonts sought the help of Gerard Croiset, a Dutch clairvoyant, who claimed the children's bodies were buried under a warehouse. The subsequent excavation, funded by public donations, turned up no evidence.

The case attracted numerous hoaxes, including letters supposedly from Jane Beaumont and "The Man" who claimed to be holding them. These letters were later determined to be a cruel joke played by a teenager at the time.

The investigation has continued sporadically over the years, with new leads emerging occasionally. In 2013, two brothers revealed that they had been hired to dig a large hole at Phipps' factory around the time of the disappearance. Despite this promising lead, the search once again yielded no results.

Theories about the children's fate have ranged from abduction and murder by a single predator to a more complex scenario involving multiple parties. Some have suggested the children were taken interstate or even overseas, though no concrete evidence supports these theories.

The disappearance of Jane, Arnna, and Grant Beaumont profoundly impacted Australian society, changing the way parents supervised their children and highlighting the potential dangers even in seemingly safe environments. The case remains open, with the South Australian Police continuing to investigate any new leads that arise.

Jim and Nancy Beaumont, who divorced many years later, never stopped searching for their children. Their hope for closure remains a poignant reminder of the enduring pain of unresolved loss. As recent as 2018, new digs and investigations were conducted, but the mystery of the Beaumont children's disappearance continues to haunt Australia.

Chapter Thirty-One

Etan Patz

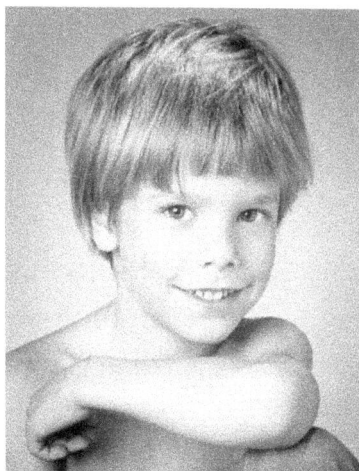

THE DISAPPEARANCE of Etan Patz on May 25, 1979, is one of the most haunting mysteries in American history. Etan, a six-year-old boy, vanished while walking to his school bus stop in the SoHo neighborhood of Lower

Manhattan. His case would captivate the nation, change the way missing children cases are handled, and remain unresolved for decades. This chapter delves into the details of the investigation, eyewitness accounts, suspects, search efforts, and the prevailing theories surrounding Etan's disappearance.

It was a misty morning when Etan Patz set off for school. For the first time, his parents, Stan and Julie Patz, allowed him to walk the two short blocks to the bus stop alone. Etan, dressed in blue pants, a blue jacket, blue sneakers, and his prized black Eastern Airlines future flight captain hat, left his home at 113 Prince Street with a dollar in his pocket to buy a soda at a nearby bodega. Julie watched as Etan walked down the street, crossing Wooster Street. Confident in his ability to navigate the short journey, she returned upstairs.

Several people saw Etan that morning. A neighbor saw him standing on the corner of Prince and Wooster Streets. A mailman also spotted him at the intersection. These would be the last confirmed sightings of Etan. Later, a witness claimed to have seen a boy matching Etan's description talking to a suspicious-looking man three blocks from the bus stop, but this lead was never confirmed.

The alarm was raised when Etan did not return home from school. Julie called the police, and a massive search ensued. The NYPD and FBI quickly became involved, scouring Lower Manhattan from 14th Street to Battery Park. Bloodhounds were brought in, police helicopters hovered overhead, and boats searched the waterways. The community rallied, distributing posters with Etan's image, and the media extensively covered the story.

One of the earliest suspects was Jose Antonio Ramos, a convicted child molester who had dated a woman who once walked Etan to school. Ramos was known to have been in the area at the time of Etan's disappearance. He admitted to being with a boy who matched Etan's description but claimed to have let him go. Despite these suspicious circumstances, there was not enough evidence to charge Ramos, though he was later found liable in a civil case filed by the Patz family.

In 1982, a photograph of a boy resembling Etan surfaced in Israel, but this lead did not pan out. Another suspect, Othniel Miller, a carpenter, was questioned after a cadaver dog detected the scent of human remains in his workshop. However, a thorough search yielded no evidence linking him to the case.

In May 2012, a significant breakthrough occurred. Pedro Hernandez, who had worked at a bodega near Etan's bus stop, confessed to strangling Etan and disposing of his body. Hernandez had a history of mental illness, and his confession was initially met with skepticism due to a lack of physical evidence. Nevertheless, he provided detailed descriptions of the events, claiming he lured Etan to the basement of the bodega by offering him a soda.

Hernandez was charged with second-degree murder and kidnapping. His defense argued that the confession was coerced and unreliable due to his mental state and low IQ. Despite these arguments, Hernandez was found guilty in 2017 and sentenced to 25 years to life in prison. This conviction provided some closure, but many questions about the case remained unanswered.

Etan Patz's disappearance had a profound impact on how missing children cases are handled in the United States. He became one of the first missing children to be featured on milk cartons, and his case led to the establishment of National Missing Children's Day on May 25. The efforts of his parents, particularly Stan Patz, who tirelessly campaigned for answers, helped bring about legislative changes and greater public awareness of child abductions.

Despite Hernandez's conviction, some continue to speculate about other potential suspects or scenarios. The fact that Etan's body was never found leaves room for doubt and alternative theories. Some believe that there might have been an accomplice or that Etan was taken by someone else entirely.

While justice was seemingly served with Hernandez's conviction, the mystery of what exactly happened to Etan Patz continues to haunt those who remember the bright, young boy who set off for school one misty morning and never returned.

Chapter Thirty-Two

Kyron Horman

KYRON HORMAN WAS an enthusiastic seven-year-old with a love for science. On the morning of June 4, 2010, he was particularly excited because Skyline Elementary School in Portland, Oregon, was hosting a science fair.

His stepmother, Terri Moulton Horman, drove him to school so he could set up his project on the Red-Eyed Tree Frog. They arrived at the school shortly after 8:00 a.m. Witnesses saw Terri and Kyron together at 8:15 a.m. near his exhibit. The school bell rang at 8:45 a.m., and Terri reported that she last saw Kyron walking towards his classroom. That was the last time he was seen.

Terri called 911 at 3:45 p.m. when Kyron did not come home on the school bus. His teacher had marked him absent, thinking he had a doctor's appointment. Realizing he had been missing for hours, an extensive search began immediately. Local law enforcement, state police, and the FBI were all involved in what became one of the largest searches in Oregon's history. Hundreds of volunteers scoured the area around Skyline Elementary and the surrounding rural areas, but there was no trace of Kyron.

Within days, the investigation shifted from a missing person case to a criminal investigation. Attention quickly turned to Terri Moulton Horman, Kyron's stepmother. Terri's behavior and inconsistencies in her story raised suspicions. She had initially claimed that after leaving the school, she spent the morning driving rural roads to soothe her infant daughter, Kiara, who had an ear infection. She later went to a 24-Hour Fitness gym at 11:39

a.m., stayed for about an hour, and then posted photos of Kyron at the science fair on Facebook around 1:21 p.m.

Terri's story had several discrepancies. Polygraph tests, which she failed multiple times, indicated deception. Eyewitnesses placed her at the school with Kyron at 8:15 a.m., but her whereabouts between 8:45 a.m. and 1:21 p.m. were not clearly accounted for. This raised further suspicion. Additionally, Terri's behavior after Kyron's disappearance was peculiar. She placed two 911 calls on June 26, 2010, one classified as a "threats" call and another involving "custody" concerns.

The case took a dramatic turn when a landscaper who worked for the Horman family came forward. He alleged that six months prior to Kyron's disappearance, Terri had offered him money to kill her husband, Kaine Horman. This revelation led Kaine to leave the family home with their daughter Kiara and file for divorce and a restraining order against Terri. The police attempted a sting operation, which led to Terri calling 911 to report someone demanding $10,000 from her. Despite these efforts, Terri was never charged, and the investigation yielded no concrete evidence linking her directly to Kyron's disappearance.

Terri had been caring for Kyron since he was an infant, following Kaine's separation from Kyron's biological mother, Desiree Young. Despite this long-term caretaking role, Desiree revealed that Terri had expressed severe resentment toward Kyron, blaming him for marital issues. Emails and testimonies suggested that Terri had a troubled relationship with both Kyron and her husband. Desiree stated that Kyron had told her several times that he wanted to come live with her, and she had attempted to get custody of him prior to his disappearance.

Eyewitnesses saw Terri and Kyron together at the school on the morning of June 4, but no one reported seeing Kyron after 8:45 a.m. The search for Kyron included extensive interviews with students, staff, and community members, and a thorough search of the school and surrounding areas. Despite the exhaustive efforts and the distribution of over 4,000 tips, no trace of Kyron was found. Law enforcement officials utilized various techniques, including search dogs, ground searches, and aerial surveillance, but they found no evidence indicating Kyron's whereabouts.

In June 2012, Desiree Young filed a civil lawsuit against Terri, accusing her of kidnapping Kyron and seeking $10 million in damages. The lawsuit was eventually dropped to avoid interfering with the ongoing criminal investigation. Despite the lack of progress, Kyron's case remains open, with the Multnomah County Sheriff's Office actively seeking new leads and conducting occasional searches based on new information. The family has continued to hold vigils and distribute flyers, keeping Kyron's disappearance in the public eye and maintaining hope for his return.

Over the years, several theories have emerged regarding Kyron's disappearance. Some believe Terri was involved due to the circumstantial evidence and her actions following the disappearance. Others speculate that Kyron could have been abducted by a stranger, although police have stated they do not believe this to be the case. Another theory suggests that someone known to the family could have taken Kyron, but no evidence has substantiated this claim. Some theories involve possible sightings of Kyron in other states, but none have led to any breakthroughs.

Kyron's disappearance has had a profound impact on his family. His father, Kaine Horman, has been vocal about the pain and uncertainty surrounding the case. He has participated in numerous media interviews, distributed flyers, and maintained a social media presence dedicated to finding Kyron. Desiree Young has also been active in advocating for her son, participating in search efforts and legal actions. The strain on the family has been immense, with ongoing tensions and public scrutiny adding to their distress.

The search for Kyron Horman continues to this day.

Law enforcement agencies remain committed to finding him, regularly reviewing the case and following up on new leads. In May 2017, a secret grand jury panel continued to hear evidence in Kyron's disappearance, and law enforcement conducted further searches along Skyline Boulevard in July of that year, but these efforts yielded no results. The case remains active and ongoing, with authorities urging anyone with information to come forward.

More than a decade has passed since Kyron Horman vanished, but the search for answers continues. The case remains one of the most perplexing and heart-wrenching in Oregon's history, marked by the enduring hope of Kyron's family and the relentless efforts of law enforcement. Until definitive answers are found, the disappearance of Kyron Horman will remain a tragic mystery that continues to captivate and sadden those who follow the case.

The case of Kyron Horman highlights the importance of community involvement in missing persons cases. The massive search efforts, volunteer participation, and media coverage have kept Kyron's story alive. The disappearance has also brought attention to the need for improved safety measures in schools and more comprehensive protocols for handling missing child cases. The legacy of Kyron's disappearance is a testament to the resilience and determination of his family and the broader community in their quest for answers and justice.

Kyron Horman's disappearance remains a haunting mystery, a case filled with unanswered questions and enduring hope. As his family and law enforcement continue their search, the story of Kyron serves as a reminder of the fragility of life and the enduring strength of a community united in the face of tragedy.

Chapter Thirty-Three

David Stone

AT JUST TWENTY-NINE YEARS OLD, David Stone seemed to have it all. A stock market analyst originally from El Paso, Texas, he had built a successful career with a major firm in La Jolla, California. Known as a likable, laid-back, and easy-going guy, David appeared to be on top of the world. However, in 1988, everything changed, leaving those who knew him struggling to understand what was happening.

During that year, David became deeply involved in the New Age movement, a surprising shift given his previous lack of interest in such things. He fully embraced the movement's ideals and frequently traveled to Sedona, Arizona, for New Age retreats and "vision quests." His excitement about these experiences was evident to his family and friends, who found his new interests odd but not necessarily concerning.

The turning point came on October 28, 1988. That evening, David hosted a party at his upscale apartment, attended by about twenty friends. The gathering was calm, with no drugs or excessive drinking. However, towards the end of the evening, David saw his close friend Anders Sjogrell handling his golf clubs. This sight triggered an uncontrollable rage in David, who attacked Anders in front of everyone, mercilessly beating him until others managed to pull him off. Anders, confused and injured, had no idea what had provoked such violence. David's behavior shocked his friends and family, who had never seen him act this way.

The next day, David seemed to realize the gravity of

his actions but couldn't explain why he had done it. He told his roommate that he was leaving town to clear his head and seek guidance on a spiritual vision quest before heading to El Paso to be the best man at a friend's wedding. David never showed up for the wedding. On the morning of October 31, he was seen in Hidalgo, Texas, about 140 miles from La Jolla, stumbling across a desert road in a t-shirt and shorts despite the chilly weather. He declined a ride from a local farmer, saying he was "looking for the beast." Other witnesses reported seeing him behaving erratically and talking to himself before he wandered off into the desert.

When David missed the wedding on November 3, his family and friends panicked. On November 5, local police found his car abandoned along a desolate stretch of Highway 80 in New Mexico, near pyramid-shaped mountains. Nearby, they discovered a pyramid of rocks surrounded by a triangle, another rock pyramid with two quarters, and David's Rolex watch. Inside the car was a business card for a man named Tony Ballesteros and a cryptic note that read, "They think the WORD is in the safe. Six knives in Rob's room. You buys your tea and you take your chances Halloween."

Searchers found more bizarre clues, including a sequence of numbers in the sand—an altered Fibonacci Sequence—and bloodhounds tracked David's scent to a spot 13 miles from his car, where they became confused and lost the trail. Tony Ballesteros, whose card was found in David's car, claimed never to have met David and suggested he might have dropped the card while hunting in the area. Despite the strange details, no signs of foul play were found.

Years passed without a trace of David until February 23, 1992, when hikers discovered human remains in a remote part of the desert near Granite Gap, New Mexico, about five miles from where David's car had been found. The remains were identified as David's, but their desiccated state made it impossible to determine the cause or time of death. Authorities labeled the death as accidental, a "death by misadventure."

To this day, we are left to wonder what really happened to David Stone. Some speculate that his interest in New Age practices and vision quests might have led to his demise, while others believe there could be a more sinister or even extraterrestrial explanation. The bizarre clues and David's uncharacteristic behavior suggest he may have been dealing with forces beyond our understanding. Whether his death was a tragic accident or something more mysterious, we may never know the full truth.

To understand the full extent of the mystery surrounding David Stone, it's essential to delve deeper into his life and the events leading up to his disappearance. David had always been an ambitious individual. His career as a stock market analyst was marked by success and recognition. He was well-respected by his colleagues and enjoyed a comfortable lifestyle in La Jolla, far from his roots in El Paso. Despite his professional success, those close to David noticed a change in him during 1988.

David's sudden interest in the New Age movement took everyone by surprise. He began attending retreats in Sedona, Arizona, and spoke enthusiastically about his experiences. He described his "vision quests" as transformative and believed they had a positive impact on his life. His family and friends, while supportive, found his new passion perplexing. They had always known David as a rational and pragmatic person, so his immersion in New Age spirituality seemed out of character.

The events of October 28, 1988, marked a significant turning point. David's party, intended to be a relaxed gathering, took a dark turn when he saw Anders Sjogrell handling his golf clubs. David's violent reaction shocked everyone present. He attacked Anders with a ferocity that was completely out of character. Friends who witnessed the incident described David as being in a trance-like state, consumed by rage. It took several people to pull him off Anders, who was left bloodied and bewildered.

The next day, David seemed to realize the gravity of his actions but couldn't explain why he had done it. He expressed deep remorse and confusion. Seeking solace, he decided to embark on a spiritual vision quest to clear his mind before attending his friend's wedding in El Paso. He assured his roommate that he needed a few days to himself and promised to return in time for the wedding.

However, David never made it to El Paso. On the morning of October 31, he was seen in Hidalgo, Texas, acting erratically and talking to himself. Witnesses described him as disoriented and unkempt, a stark contrast to his usual composed self. He declined offers of help, insisting that he was "looking for the beast." His behavior puzzled those who saw him, but no one realized the gravity of the situation at the time.

When David failed to show up for the wedding on November 3, his family and friends knew something was terribly wrong. Their worst fears were confirmed when, on November 5, local police found his car abandoned on a remote stretch of Highway 80 in New Mexico. The car was near pyramid-shaped mountains, and searchers discovered a series of cryptic clues. A pyramid of rocks surrounded by a triangle, another rock pyramid with two quarters and David's Rolex watch, and a cryptic note in his car all added to the mystery.

The note read, "They think the WORD is in the safe. Six knives in Rob's room. You buys your tea and you take your chances Halloween." This cryptic message, combined with the strange symbols and altered Fibonacci Sequence found in the sand, baffled investigators. Bloodhounds tracked David's scent to a spot 13 miles from his car, where the trail abruptly ended. The dogs became confused and were unable to follow the scent any further.

Tony Ballesteros, whose business card was found in David's car, was questioned by police. He claimed never to have met David and suggested he might have accidentally dropped the card while hunting in the area. Despite thorough investigations, no evidence of foul play was found. The case left even the most experienced investigators scratching their heads.

Years passed without any sign of David until February 23, 1992, when hikers stumbled upon human remains in a remote part of the desert near Granite Gap, New Mexico. The remains were identified as David's, but the condition of the body made it impossible to determine the cause or time of death. Authorities labeled the death as accidental, attributing it to the harsh desert environment. However, the unanswered questions and bizarre clues left many wondering if there was more to the story.

The case of David Stone remains one of the most perplexing mysteries. His sudden immersion in the New Age movement, the violent outburst at the party, and the cryptic clues found after his disappearance suggest a complex and potentially otherworldly narrative. Some speculate that David's interest in New Age practices might have led him into dangerous territory, while others believe he may have encountered forces beyond our understanding.

David's story continues to captivate those who hear it. The combination of strange symbols, cryptic messages, and his unexplained disappearance has led to numerous theories, ranging from psychological breakdowns to encounters with extraterrestrial beings. The lack of concrete answers only adds to the intrigue, leaving us to wonder what really happened to David Stone in the desert all those years ago.

In the realm of unsolved mysteries and paranormal investigations, David's case stands out for its unique blend of spiritual, psychological, and potentially extraterrestrial elements. Whether his death was the result of a tragic accident, a mental breakdown, or something far more mysterious, it remains a compelling story that challenges our understanding of reality.

Chapter Thirty-Four

Jennifer Kesse

JENNIFER KESSE's disappearance on January 24, 2006, remains one of the most baffling cases in recent history. Despite extensive investigations and numerous leads, the 24-year-old financial analyst vanished without a trace, leaving behind a trail of questions and few answers. This chapter delves into the details surrounding her disappearance, the police investigation, suspects, eyewitness accounts, search efforts, and prevailing theories.

Jennifer Kesse, a University of Central Florida graduate, was living at the Mosaic at Millenia, a condo complex in Orlando, Florida. She was last heard from on the evening of January 23, 2006, after a phone call with her boyfriend, Rob Allen. Jennifer had returned from a trip to the Virgin Islands with Rob just days before and was preparing for another day at work as a financial analyst at a timeshare company in Ocoee, Florida.

On the morning of January 24, Jennifer failed to show up for work. Concerned, her employer contacted her parents, who quickly realized something was wrong when they couldn't reach her. Jennifer's parents, Drew and Joyce Kesse, along with her brother, Logan, and his friend, Travis, went to her condo. They found her car missing, but there were no signs of a struggle inside her apartment.

Three days later, on January 27, Jennifer's black 2004 Chevy Malibu was found abandoned at the Huntington on the Green apartment complex, about a mile from her home. Surveillance footage showed an unidentified person parking the car around noon on the day Jennifer disappeared. Unfortunately, the footage was grainy, and the person's face was obscured by a fence post, making identification impossible.

The Orlando Police Department (OPD) launched an extensive investigation. They initially focused on Jennifer's immediate circle, including her boyfriend and ex-boyfriend, both of whom were cleared of any involvement. Attention then shifted to the construction workers at her condo complex, as Jennifer had previously expressed concerns about their behavior, noting that they often catcalled and harassed her.

Despite extensive interviews and searches, the construction workers were never thoroughly vetted due to language barriers and lack of solid leads. The investigation also included forensic examinations of Jennifer's car and condo. A small amount of DNA and a latent fingerprint were found in the car, but these provided no significant breakthroughs.

Eyewitness accounts were scarce. The most significant lead was the surveillance footage from Huntington on the Green, but the unidentified person seen in the video remained elusive. The FBI and NASA were brought in to enhance the video, but they could only determine that the person was between 5'3" and 5'5" tall.

A search dog tracked Jennifer's scent from her car back to her condo complex, suggesting that her abductor might have returned to the scene. This finding, however, led to no further evidence.

Over the years, several theories have emerged regarding Jennifer's disappearance:

1. Abduction by a Stranger: The most widely accepted theory is that Jennifer was abducted by a stranger, possibly one of the construction workers at her complex. The fact that her car was found so close to her home supports the idea that her abductor was familiar with the area.

2. Human Trafficking: Some speculate that Jennifer may have been a victim of human trafficking, though this theory is considered less likely by investigators and her family.

3. Voluntary Disappearance: While some have suggested that Jennifer might have disappeared voluntarily, her family and friends strongly dismiss this idea, citing her strong ties to her family, her steady job, and her general behavior leading up to her disappearance.

Frustrated with the OPD's handling of the case, the Kesse family sued the department to gain access to the case files. They hired private investigators and a team of retired law enforcement officers to review the files, leading to the discovery of previously unknown details, such as potential signs of a struggle in Jennifer's car.

In 2022, the Florida Department of Law Enforcement (FDLE) took over the case, promising a fresh start to the investigation. The Kesse family remains hopeful that new techniques, including advanced DNA testing, might finally provide answers.

Jennifer's disappearance has attracted national attention, with numerous media outlets covering the case and publicizing the search for new leads. The family has maintained a strong online presence, using social media and a dedicated website to keep Jennifer's story alive and encourage anyone with information to come forward.

The Kesse family has offered substantial rewards for information leading to Jennifer's whereabouts, including a $1 million reward offered by her employer, though it expired without any leads.

The disappearance of Jennifer Kesse remains an agonizing mystery. Despite the extensive efforts of law enforcement, private investigators, and her determined family, Jennifer's fate is still unknown. The case stands as a haunting reminder of the many missing person cases that remain unresolved, urging continued vigilance and innovation in investigative methods. The hope is that one day, the truth will emerge, providing closure to Jennifer's family and ensuring that justice is served.

Chapter Thirty-Five

Arjen Kamphuis

ARJEN KAMPHUIS, a renowned Dutch cybersecurity expert and WikiLeaks associate, vanished under mysterious circumstances in August 2018 while on holiday in Norway. His disappearance has sparked numerous theories and speculation, ranging from an accidental death to foul play involving international intelligence agencies. This chapter explores the details of his disappearance, the police investigation, eyewitness accounts, and the prevailing theories.

Arjen Kamphuis was a prominent figure in the field of cybersecurity, known for his work on information security and privacy. He had a notable career advising governments, corporations, and activists on preventing hacking attacks and maintaining digital security. Kamphuis also had connections to WikiLeaks and had collaborated with Julian Assange and other figures in the transparency movement.

Kamphuis checked out of his hotel in Bodø, Norway, on August 20, 2018, with plans to travel to Trondheim by train. He was scheduled to fly back to the Netherlands on August 22 but never boarded his flight. His disappearance was reported after he failed to return, prompting a widespread search and investigation by Norwegian authorities, assisted by Dutch investigators.

The initial search efforts were extensive, involving police, the Red Cross, and local volunteers. A key breakthrough came when a fisherman found some of Kamphuis's belongings, including his ID card, floating in the water near the Skjerstad Fjord, approximately 50 kilometers from Bodø. A damaged kayak believed to belong to Kamphuis was also recovered in the same area.

Despite these findings, the mystery deepened when, ten days after his disappearance, Kamphuis's mobile phone was activated near Vikeså, a location 1,700 kilometers from where his belongings were found. The phone was switched on for a brief period before the SIM card was replaced with a German one, adding to the enigma of his disappearance.

1. Accidental Death: The most widely accepted theory by Norwegian police is that Kamphuis suffered an accident while kayaking in the fjord. The rough waters and the damaged kayak suggest that he might have drowned after capsizing. Despite extensive searches, his body has never been found, leading to ongoing speculation.

2. Voluntary Disappearance: Some believe that Kamphuis, who had occasionally expressed a desire to disappear and possessed the skills to do so, might have orchestrated his own disappearance. His knowledge of digital security could have enabled him to evade detection if he chose to start a new life elsewhere.

3. Foul Play: Given Kamphuis's work and associations, there are theories suggesting foul play involving

intelligence agencies. His connection to WikiLeaks and his outspoken stance on privacy rights have fueled suspicions that he might have been targeted by entities seeking to silence him. Supporters of this theory point to the unexplained activation of his phone and the strategic placement of his belongings as potential evidence of a covert operation.

4. Murder: Another possibility considered by investigators is that Kamphuis was murdered. This theory is bolstered by the unusual circumstances of his disappearance and the subsequent discovery of his phone far from the original search area. However, no concrete evidence has emerged to support this scenario.

In the days following Kamphuis's disappearance, several unconfirmed sightings were reported. Some witnesses claimed to have seen a man matching his description in the vicinity of Bodø, but none of these accounts could be verified. The activation of his phone in Vikeså added another layer of confusion, leading to speculation about his movements during the ten-day period.

The case attracted significant media attention and public interest, partly due to Kamphuis's association with WikiLeaks. Various conspiracy theories emerged, with some suggesting involvement by the CIA, Russian intelligence, or other clandestine agencies. WikiLeaks itself highlighted the mysterious nature of Kamphuis's disappearance, further fueling speculation and debate.

The disappearance of Arjen Kamphuis remains unresolved, with several plausible theories but no definitive answers. While the Norwegian police concluded that he likely died in a kayaking accident, the absence of his body and the mysterious activation of his phone leave room for doubt and ongoing speculation. Kamphuis's case underscores the complexities and uncertainties involved in missing persons investigations, especially when the individual in question is a high-profile figure with sensitive connections and expertise.

Kamphuis's legacy as a cybersecurity expert and privacy advocate continues to be remembered by his colleagues and the broader community. His disappearance serves as a stark reminder of the vulnerabilities faced by those working on the frontlines of digital security and privacy.

Chapter Thirty-Six

Ann Marie Burr

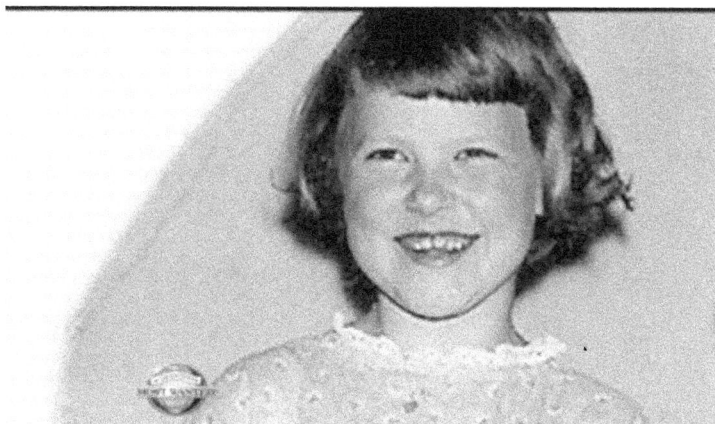

On August 31, 1961, the quiet neighborhood of North Tacoma, Washington, was shaken by the sudden and unexplained disappearance of eight-year-old Ann Marie Burr. The case has become one of the most enduring mysteries in American history, baffling investigators and haunting the local community for over six decades. This chapter delves into the circumstances surrounding Ann Marie's disappearance, the details of the investigation, eyewitness accounts, and the various theories that have emerged over the years.

The Burr family lived in a modest home at 3009 North 14th Street in Tacoma. Donald Burr was a respected local lawyer, and Beverly Burr was a devoted mother to their four children: Ann Marie, Mary, Greg, and Julie. Ann Marie, the eldest, was a bright, sociable child who was looking forward to starting third grade at Grant Elementary School. The Burrs were a typical middle-class family, involved in their community and well-liked by their neighbors.

In the days leading up to her disappearance, Ann Marie had requested to spend the night of August 30 at a friend's house. However, her mother, Beverly, had declined, wanting to maintain a routine as the new school year approached. This decision, in hindsight, would be a source of great anguish for the Burr family.

The night of August 30, 1961, was stormy, with heavy rain and strong winds battering the Burr household. Around midnight, Ann Marie brought her younger sister, Mary, to their parents' bedroom. Mary, who had a broken arm in a cast, was uncomfortable and needed attention. Beverly comforted Mary and sent both girls back to bed.

At approximately 5:00 AM, Beverly woke with a sense of unease. She checked on the children and found Ann Marie's bed empty. A quick search of the house revealed disturbing signs: a living room window, usually kept slightly open for a TV antenna wire, was fully open; a garden bench had been placed beneath the window; and the front door, which had been locked, was now ajar.

Beverly immediately woke Donald, and they began searching the house and yard for any sign of their daughter. When their initial search proved fruitless, they called the police. Detectives Tony Zatkovich and Ted Strand arrived at the Burr home around 6:45 AM. They meticulously examined the scene, finding a small footprint on the garden bench and a red thread snagged on the window sill.

The detectives interviewed Beverly and Donald, who recounted hearing strange noises in their yard during the night and in the days leading up to the disappearance. Neighbors also reported seeing a peeping Tom in the area, but no one could provide a detailed description.

The search for Ann Marie Burr quickly escalated into one of the largest manhunts in Tacoma's history.

Over 1,500 people were interviewed in the first twelve days following her disappearance. Law enforcement, along with volunteers from the community, combed the city and surrounding areas. National Guardsmen, police officers, and even divers searched sewers, creeks, and the bay, but no trace of Ann Marie was found.

The investigation focused on several potential suspects. One teenage boy, who lived nearby and had shown interest in Ann Marie, was subjected to a polygraph test. Initially, he failed but later passed a subsequent test. Another suspect was a relative of the Burrs, who would later be convicted of child molestation. Despite extensive questioning and investigation, these leads did not result in any significant breakthroughs.

One of the most enduring and chilling theories regarding Ann Marie Burr's disappearance involves the infamous serial killer Ted Bundy. At the time of Ann Marie's disappearance, Bundy was a 14-year-old boy living just two miles from the Burr home. He delivered newspapers in the neighborhood, and there were rumors that Ann Marie knew him and sometimes followed him on his route.

Bundy's later criminal activities and his proximity to the Burr family led many to suspect that he might have been involved in Ann Marie's disappearance. When Bundy was arrested in the late 1970s for a series of brutal murders, investigators began to look into his possible connection to the Burr case. Bundy himself alternately denied and hinted at his involvement, further complicating the investigation.

In a 1986 letter to Bundy, Beverly Burr asked him directly about her daughter. Bundy replied, denying any involvement and stating, "First and foremost, I do not know what happened to your daughter Ann Marie. I had nothing to do with her disappearance". Despite this denial, Bundy's ambiguous statements to other investigators and his history of deceit have kept him as a prime suspect in the eyes of many.

Throughout the investigation, various eyewitness accounts and leads emerged. Some neighbors reported seeing a man peering into the Burrs' windows on the night of the disappearance. Others mentioned hearing strange noises in the neighborhood. A service station employee in Manitoba, Canada, claimed to have seen a girl matching Ann Marie's description with a man and a woman who spoke sharply to her. This lead, like many others, did not yield any concrete results.

In the winter of 1964, law enforcement attempted to arrest Ralph Everett Larkee in Portland, Oregon, in connection with the kidnapping of another girl. Larkee, who was considered a suspect in Ann Marie's disappearance, committed suicide before he could be apprehended.

Over the years, various theories have been proposed to explain Ann Marie's disappearance:

1. Stranger Abduction: This theory posits that Ann Marie was taken by a stranger who had been watching the house and knew the layout well enough to enter quietly. The small footprint and the bench placement suggest a young or small-statured individual.

2. Ted Bundy's Involvement: Bundy's proximity to the Burr family and his later confessions to similar crimes make him a plausible suspect. His ambiguous statements and the nature of his crimes align with the circumstances of Ann Marie's disappearance.

3. Kidnapping by an Acquaintance: Another theory is that Ann Marie was taken by someone she knew, possibly a neighbor or family acquaintance. The lack of a struggle and the open door suggest she might have trusted her abductor enough to let them in or follow them willingly.

4. Family Involvement: Although less likely, some have speculated about the possibility of family involvement. Beverly and Donald Burr were subjected to polygraph tests and extensive questioning, but no evidence was found to implicate them.

Despite the exhaustive efforts of law enforcement, the Burr family, and the community, Ann Marie Burr's case remains unsolved. Over the decades, various individuals have come forward with tips and potential leads, but none have led to a resolution. The Burr family received numerous letters and calls from people claiming to have information about Ann Marie, but most of these turned out to be false leads or cruel hoaxes.

The case has left a lasting impact on the Tacoma community and has become a focal point for discussions about child abduction and the need for improved safety measures. The disappearance of Ann Marie Burr remains a tragic and unresolved chapter in the history of the Pacific Northwest.

The disappearance of Ann Marie Burr is a tragic and enduring mystery. The case has left a lasting impact on the Tacoma community and continues to capture the interest of true crime enthusiasts and investigators. While various theories and suspects have been explored, including the possible involvement of Ted Bundy, Ann Marie's fate remains unknown.

As time passes, the hope of finding definitive answers dims, but the memory of Ann Marie Burr endures. Her case serves as a poignant reminder of the pain and uncertainty faced by families of missing persons and the importance of continuing to search for the truth, no matter how elusive it may be.

In the absence of closure, the story of Ann Marie Burr stands as a testament to the enduring love and determination of her family and the relentless pursuit of justice by those who seek to uncover the truth behind her disappearance.

Chapter Thirty-Seven

Michaela Garecht

ON NOVEMBER 19, 1988, nine-year-old Michaela Joy Garecht was abducted from a supermarket parking lot in

Hayward, California. This chapter explores the detailed account of Michaela's disappearance, the investigation that ensued, and the numerous theories and suspects that emerged over the years. Despite decades of relentless search and investigative efforts, her case remains unsolved, leaving a lingering mystery and an enduring quest for justice.

Michaela Garecht was a cheerful, blonde-haired girl living in the suburbs of Hayward, California. On the morning of November 19, 1988, Michaela and her friend Katrina Rodriguez decided to ride their scooters to the Rainbow Market, a local store just two blocks from Michaela's home. It was a typical Saturday morning, and the girls were looking forward to buying some snacks and enjoying their time together.

After making their purchases, they exited the store to find that Michaela's friend's scooter had been moved. It was now closer to a vehicle in the parking lot. Without any hesitation, Michaela walked over to retrieve it. As she bent down to pick up the scooter, a man grabbed her by the waist and forced her into his car. Rodriguez, who witnessed the abduction, was momentarily paralyzed by shock. She then ran into the store and frantically asked a clerk to call 911. Michaela's screams echoed in the parking lot, but the abductor sped away with her in a tan or gold-colored sedan.

The Hayward Police Department responded swiftly. Witnesses described the abductor as a Caucasian male, aged 18 to 24, with a slender build, long dirty blonde hair, and a face pockmarked with acne. He was driving an older model, battered sedan, possibly a four-door vehicle with damage to the front bumper and cement splatters on the sides. Despite the detailed description, the abductor managed to vanish, and Michaela's whereabouts remained unknown.

The initial investigation involved extensive searches of the local area, including nearby fields and waterways. Flyers with Michaela's photo and the suspect's description were distributed widely. The FBI was soon involved, and they employed helicopters and airplanes in their search efforts. Over 5,000 tips were received in the first year, but none led to Michaela.

Katrina Rodriguez's eyewitness account was crucial in forming the initial suspect sketch. The clerk at the Rainbow Market, however, initially misidentified the man, describing a different individual she had seen in the parking lot earlier. It took two days for the police to correct the description, which hindered the early stages of the investigation. Rodriguez described the suspect as having long, blonde hair, blue eyes, and a pockmarked face. This revised sketch was disseminated across the nation.

As the investigation progressed, several suspects emerged:

1. Tim Bindner: Bindner was an eccentric individual who often involved himself in the search efforts for missing children. He became a person of interest not only in Michaela's case but also in the disappearances of Amber Swartz, Ilene Misheloff, and Amanda Campbell. Bindner's unusual behavior, including sending letters to the families of missing children and visiting their graves, made him a suspect. However, despite extensive investigation, no concrete evidence linked him to Michaela's disappearance, and he maintained his innocence.

2. Phillip Garrido: The 2009 recovery of Jaycee Lee Dugard, who had been held captive for 18 years, led investigators to consider her captor, Phillip Garrido, as a possible suspect. Garrido's proximity to Hayward and the similarity in the modus operandi—abducting girls in broad daylight—prompted a thorough investigation. However, no evidence was found connecting him to Michaela's case.

3. Speed Freak Killers: Wesley Shermantine and Loren Herzog, known as the Speed Freak Killers, were linked to numerous murders in Northern California. In 2012, Shermantine directed investigators to

an abandoned well where they found bone fragments belonging to several individuals. DNA testing ruled out Michaela as one of the victims, but the case renewed public interest and brought new leads.

4. David Misch: In December 2020, David Misch, a convicted murderer, was charged with Michaela's abduction and murder. Misch's involvement came to light when a fingerprint found on Michaela's scooter was reexamined using modern technology and matched to him. Misch, who was in the area at the time of the abduction and matched the suspect's description, is now awaiting trial. This breakthrough provided a significant development in the case, but Michaela's remains have yet to be found.

The search for Michaela Garecht has spanned over three decades. Her mother, Sharon Murch, has been a tireless advocate, maintaining a blog to document case updates and her personal journey. Murch's determination to find her daughter has kept the case alive in the public eye and has been instrumental in ensuring that the investigation continues.

In the years following the abduction, the Hayward Police Department and the FBI have pursued numerous leads. Tips and potential sightings have been investigated across the United States and internationally.

Despite these efforts, Michaela has not been found, and her case remains one of the most perplexing mysteries in American history.

Michaela's disappearance garnered significant media attention. Her case was featured on national television shows, including "America's Most Wanted" and "Unsolved Mysteries." The widespread coverage kept the public informed and generated thousands of tips, although none resulted in Michaela's recovery. The media played a crucial role in maintaining public interest and keeping the pressure on law enforcement to continue their efforts.

Michaela's abduction had a profound impact on the Hayward community and beyond. The fear and uncertainty following her disappearance led to increased awareness and caution among parents and children. Community members organized vigils and events to raise awareness and support the Garecht family. The case also highlighted the need for improved safety measures and protocols to protect children from similar tragedies.

The identification of David Misch as a suspect in Michaela's abduction and murder was a significant development. Misch's criminal history and the forensic evidence linking him to the crime have brought renewed hope for justice. As of now, Misch is awaiting trial, and the Garecht family, along with the community, remains hopeful that this will lead to answers and closure.

The legal proceedings against Misch have also raised important questions about the handling of cold cases and the advancements in forensic technology that can aid in solving them. The ability to reexamine old evidence with new techniques has proven crucial in cases like Michaela's and underscores the importance of preserving and revisiting evidence in unsolved cases.

The disappearance of Michaela Garecht is a tragic and haunting mystery that continues to resonate. The relentless pursuit of answers by her family, law enforcement, and the community serves as a testament to their enduring hope and determination. While the road to justice has been long and fraught with challenges, the case remains active, and the search for Michaela continues.

As advancements in technology and forensic science progress, there is hope that more cold cases like Michaela's can be resolved. The commitment to finding the truth and bringing closure to families remains a driving force behind these efforts. Michaela's story is a reminder of the importance of vigilance, community support, and the relentless pursuit of justice in the face of uncertainty.

Michaela Garecht's disappearance remains one of

the most poignant and unresolved cases in American history. The abduction of a young girl in broad daylight, the extensive but ultimately fruitless search efforts, and the emergence of numerous suspects and theories have all contributed to the enduring mystery surrounding her case.

The recent developments with the charging of David Misch offer a glimmer of hope for resolution. As the legal process unfolds, the Garecht family and the public await answers that have been elusive for over three decades. The quest for justice and the hope for Michaela's return continue to inspire those involved in the investigation and serve as a beacon of perseverance and resilience.

In the end, Michaela's story is not just about a tragic disappearance but also about the unwavering love and determination of a family and a community. It is a story that reminds us of the importance of never giving up and of always seeking the truth, no matter how long it takes or how difficult the journey may be.

Chapter Thirty-Eight

Steven Koecher

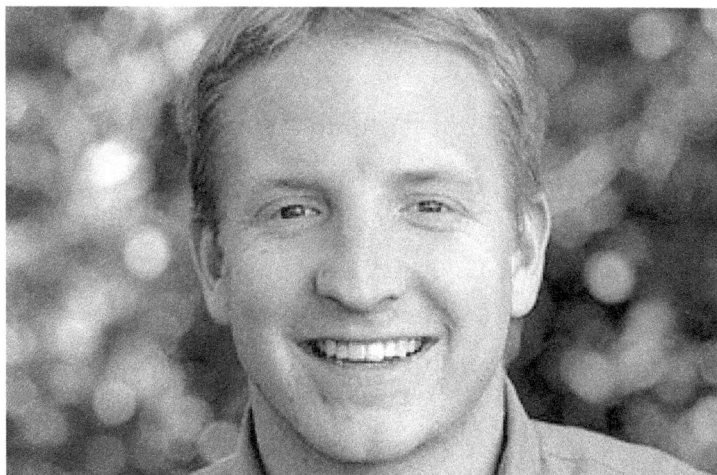

STEVEN THELL KOECHER, a 30-year-old man from St. George, Utah, vanished under perplexing circumstances in December 2009. His disappearance, which has captivated investigators and the public alike, remains unsolved. This chapter explores the timeline of events leading up to Steven's disappearance, the subsequent investigation, and the theories that have emerged in the years since.

Steven Koecher was born on November 1, 1979, in Amarillo, Texas. He was active in the Boy Scouts of America, achieving the rank of Eagle Scout. After graduating from Amarillo High School in 1998, Steven attended Ricks College (now Brigham Young University-Idaho) and later graduated from the University of Utah. Steven, a devout member of the Church of Jesus Christ of Latter-day Saints (LDS), was known for his strong faith and involvement in church activities.

In early 2009, Steven moved from Salt Lake City to St. George, Utah, in search of employment opportunities. He had previously worked for the online division of the Salt Lake Tribune but struggled to find stable work after moving. By December 2009, Steven was employed part-time with a window-washing company, but his financial situation remained precarious.

On December 10, 2009, Steven made an unexplained trip from St. George to Las Vegas, Nevada, approximately 120 miles away. He returned the same day without informing anyone of the purpose of his visit. Two days later, on December 12, he set out again, this time heading towards Henderson, Nevada, a suburb of Las Vegas.

Security footage captured Steven's white 2003 Chevrolet Cavalier driving into a cul-de-sac on Savannah Springs Avenue in the Sun City Anthem neighborhood of Henderson at 11:54 AM on December 13. Six minutes later, Steven was seen walking down the sidewalk, carrying a small object that appeared to be a file folder or portfolio. This was the last confirmed sighting of him.

Steven's family reported him missing on December 17, 2009, after realizing they had not heard from him in several days. His car, found in the upscale residential neighborhood of Sun City Anthem, contained his shaving kit, coats, pillows, blankets, and Christmas gifts he had purchased a few days earlier. Missing, however, were his wallet, cell phone, and driver's license. His laptop and cell phone charger were left behind at his apartment in St. George.

Steven's cell phone continued to ping off various towers in the Henderson area for several days after his disappearance. Around 5:00 PM on December 13, his phone pinged near Arroyo Grande Boulevard and American Pacific Drive, over 10 miles from where his car was found. Two hours later, another ping was recorded near the Whitney Ranch subdivision. The next morning, at around 6:00 AM, the phone pinged near the interchange of Interstate 515 and Russell Road. The phone remained in that vicinity for two days before its signal was lost, presumably because the battery died.

Several residents of the Sun City Anthem neighborhood reported seeing Steven walking through the area. However, these sightings provided little information about his intentions or destination. One resident recalled an odd conversation with Steven, in which he seemed to be looking for someone or something, but the details were vague and did not lead to any substantial clues.

One theory is that Steven traveled to Henderson seeking employment. He was known to be actively job-hunting at the time, and the trip may have been related to a potential job opportunity. However, there is no concrete evidence to support this theory, and his family believes he would have informed them if he had a job lead.

Another theory suggests that Steven may have voluntarily disappeared to escape financial troubles and personal issues. Although he was struggling financially, his family insists that he would not have left without telling anyone. Additionally, Steven had purchased Christmas gifts for his family, indicating he intended to see them during the holiday season.

The possibility of foul play has been considered,

particularly given the unusual circumstances of his disappearance and the location of his abandoned car. However, no evidence of a struggle or foul play was found in his car or at the scene. The scattered pings of his cell phone could suggest he was moving around the area willingly or being transported by someone.

Steven's disappearance occurred around the same time as the high-profile case of Susan Powell, who vanished from West Valley City, Utah, on December 7, 2009. Some speculated that the cases might be connected due to the similarities in timing and location. However, investigators found no evidence linking the two cases or indicating that Steven and Susan knew each other.

Some have theorized that Steven may have been experiencing a personal crisis, possibly related to his religious beliefs or financial struggles. This theory posits that he might have wandered off into the desert or another remote area to contemplate his situation or even end his life. Despite extensive searches of the surrounding areas, no trace of Steven has been found.

Despite numerous searches, interviews, and investigations by both police and private detectives, Steven's whereabouts remain unknown. His family has continued to search for him, maintaining hope that he might still be found. They have distributed flyers, conducted searches, and appeared on various media outlets to keep his case in the public eye.

In 2015, a new theory emerged, sparking a renewed search effort. Volunteers from Red Rock Search and Rescue, a local group, combed the areas around Henderson and beyond, but no new evidence was uncovered.

The disappearance of Steven Koecher remains one of the most baffling missing persons cases in recent history. The lack of concrete evidence, conflicting theories, and the mystery of his final movements have left his family and investigators searching for answers. As the years pass, the hope of finding Steven diminishes, but his family continues to seek closure, holding on to the belief that one day they will discover what happened to their beloved son and brother.

The enigma of Steven Koecher's disappearance is a stark reminder of the complexities and uncertainties that can accompany missing persons cases. It highlights the need for continued efforts in search and rescue operations, the importance of maintaining public awareness, and the enduring hope of finding the missing, no matter how much time has passed.

Chapter Thirty-Nine

Jim Sullivan

JIM SULLIVAN, a talented but obscure singer-songwriter, vanished without a trace in the New Mexico desert in March 1975. Despite extensive search efforts and numerous theories, his disappearance remains one of the most perplexing mysteries in rock and roll history. This chapter explores the details surrounding Sullivan's life, disappearance, and the enduring enigma that continues to captivate those who delve into his story.

James Anthony Sullivan was born on August 13, 1939, in Nebraska, the seventh son of a blue-collar Irish-American family. The Sullivans moved to California during World War II, where Jim grew up and developed a passion for music. He played guitar in various rock groups before moving to Los Angeles to pursue a career in music. There, he became part of the vibrant Malibu music scene, mingling with celebrities like Dennis Hopper and Harry Dean Stanton.

In 1969, Sullivan released his debut album, *U.F.O.*, on a small label founded by his friend Al Dobbs. The album, featuring members of the famed Wrecking Crew, was a unique blend of folk-rock with psychedelic undertones, and its lyrics often explored themes of alienation and desert landscapes. Despite its artistic merit, *U.F.O.* received little commercial success.

Sullivan's second album, *Jim Sullivan*, released in 1972 by Playboy Records, also failed to gain traction. By 1975, Sullivan's career had stalled, his marriage was in trouble, and he struggled with a drinking problem. He decided to move to Nashville in hopes of reviving his music career and promised his wife and son they would join him once he got settled.

On March 4, 1975, Sullivan left Los Angeles in his Volkswagen Beetle, headed for Nashville. His journey took a mysterious turn when he reached Santa Rosa, New Mexico. According to police reports, Sullivan was stopped by local authorities for swerving on the road. After passing a sobriety test, he checked into the La Mesa Motel. The next day, his car was found abandoned at a ranch 26 miles south of Santa Rosa.

Sullivan was reportedly seen at the remote ranch owned by the Gennitti family, where he seemed disoriented but not overtly distressed. His car contained his guitar, clothes, wallet, and a box of his unsold records. The motel room showed no signs of being slept in, and the key was found locked inside. Despite extensive searches by local law enforcement and Sullivan's family, no trace of him was ever found.

In the months following his disappearance, there were several unconfirmed sightings of Sullivan in the area. However, none of these led to any substantial clues. A decomposed body found in the vicinity was initially thought to be Sullivan, but it was later determined not to be him.

Over the years, numerous theories have emerged regarding Jim Sullivan's disappearance:

1. Suicide: Some speculate that Sullivan, overwhelmed by his personal and professional failures, may have taken his own life. However, no evidence supports this theory, and those who knew him described him as having a strong will to overcome his difficulties.

2. Foul Play: Given Sullivan's connections in the music industry and his claims of stolen music, some theorize that he may have run afoul of dangerous individuals. There is no concrete evidence to support involvement by the Mafia or other criminal elements, but the theory persists due to the mysterious circumstances of his disappearance.

3. Alien Abduction: One of the more outlandish theories, fueled by the themes of his album *U.F.O.*, suggests that Sullivan was abducted by extraterrestrials. While this theory is mostly speculative, it has captured the imaginations of many due to the eeriness of his music and the desert setting of his disappearance.

4. Accidental Death: Another plausible theory is that Sullivan wandered into the desert, became disoriented, and succumbed to the harsh environment. The

New Mexico desert is vast and unforgiving, and it is possible that his remains were simply never found.

5. Voluntary Disappearance: Some believe that Sullivan may have intentionally disappeared to start a new life. However, this seems unlikely given his strong ties to his family and his plans to bring them to Nashville once he was established.

Jim Sullivan's music gained a cult following after his disappearance, particularly his album *U.F.O.*, which was reissued by Light in the Attic Records in 2010. The reissue brought renewed interest in his work and the mystery surrounding his disappearance. Matt Sullivan (no relation), the founder of Light in the Attic Records, conducted extensive research into Jim's life and disappearance, but no definitive answers emerged.

Sullivan's music, characterized by its haunting melodies and introspective lyrics, continues to resonate with listeners. His disappearance has been the subject of numerous articles, podcasts, and documentaries, each exploring different aspects of his life and the enduring mystery of his fate.

The disappearance of Jim Sullivan remains one of rock and roll's greatest mysteries. Despite exhaustive investigations and numerous theories, no conclusive evidence has ever been found to explain what happened to him in the New Mexico desert. Sullivan's story is a poignant reminder of the fragility of life and the enduring allure of unanswered questions. As his music continues to find new audiences, the search for answers about his fate goes on, keeping the legacy of Jim Sullivan alive.

Chapter Forty

Sneha Anne Philip

THE CASE of Dr. Sneha Anne Philip is one of the most intriguing and enigmatic disappearances linked to the tragic events of September 11, 2001. A young physician with a promising career, Sneha was last seen on

September 10, 2001, in Lower Manhattan. Her disappearance has sparked numerous theories, blending personal turmoil, potential foul play, and the chaos of the 9/11 attacks. This chapter examines the details surrounding her disappearance, police findings, eyewitness accounts, and prevailing theories.

Sneha Anne Philip, born in Kerala, India, was a third-year medical resident living in Battery Park City, New York, with her husband, Dr. Ron Lieberman. By all accounts, Sneha was a vibrant and intelligent woman, yet her life in the months leading up to her disappearance was marked by significant challenges.

Earlier in 2001, Sneha was dismissed from her residency at Cabrini Medical Center due to repeated tardiness and alleged alcohol-related issues. This dismissal deeply affected her, contributing to a period of personal turmoil. Despite this setback, she secured another position at St. Vincent's Medical Center on Staten Island but faced similar issues, including a suspension for missing a meeting with a substance abuse counselor.

Sneha's personal life was also complicated. Her nights out at lesbian bars, sometimes with rough clientele, and her occasional overnight absences without informing her husband, led to tension in her marriage. An incident where Sneha accused a colleague of sexual assault, which led to her arrest for filing a false report, further strained her relationships and added to her legal troubles.

On September 10, 2001, Sneha spent a seemingly ordinary day. She was seen on surveillance footage shopping at a department store near her apartment. She bought several items, including lingerie, a dress, bed linen, and shoes. This shopping trip was the last confirmed sighting of Sneha. That evening, she did not return home, but her husband did not immediately worry, as her overnight absences were not unusual.

The morning of September 11, 2001, Ron Lieberman left for work, assuming Sneha would return soon. When the first plane struck the North Tower of the World Trade Center, just two blocks from their apartment, Ron tried to contact Sneha but was unsuccessful. As news of the attack spread, he feared the worst and began searching for her among friends, family, and hospitals.

The New York Police Department (NYPD) initially struggled to investigate Sneha's disappearance due to the overwhelming chaos following the 9/11 attacks. When they did investigate, they uncovered troubling details about her personal life, suggesting she might have been elsewhere or already deceased when the towers fell.

According to the police, Sneha's recent behavior, including her nights out and troubled professional life, painted a picture of a woman in distress. They suggested various possibilities, including that she might have used the chaos of 9/11 to escape her life or that she met with foul play during one of her nights out.

1. Victim of 9/11: Sneha's family believes she perished in the 9/11 attacks. Given her proximity to the World Trade Center and her medical training, they speculate she might have rushed to help the injured and died in the collapse. This theory is supported by her compassionate nature and dedication to her profession.

2. Foul Play: Another theory is that Sneha met with foul play. Her frequenting of bars and staying out overnight could have exposed her to dangerous situations. The police report also hinted at possible altercations with strangers or acquaintances that might have led to her disappearance.

3. Voluntary Disappearance: Some speculate that Sneha used the 9/11 attacks as an opportunity to escape her increasingly complicated life. However, this theory is undermined by the lack of evidence showing she made any preparations for a new life. Her essential belongings, such as her glasses, passport, and credit cards, were left behind, and there was no activity on her remaining credit card.

In the years following her disappearance, legal battles ensued regarding Sneha's official status as a 9/11 victim. Initially, she was listed among the victims, but in 2004, the city medical examiner removed her name, citing insufficient evidence that she was at the World Trade Center on 9/11.

In 2003, Ron Lieberman filed a petition to have Sneha declared a victim of the attacks, but a Surrogate Court judge ruled that she officially died on September 10, 2004, three years after her disappearance. This ruling devastated her family, who maintained that she likely died heroically on 9/11.

Sneha's family strongly disputes many of the police findings. They argue that her dismissal from Cabrini Medical Center was due to her whistleblowing on racial and sexual bias, not alcohol issues. They also reject the claim that she had serious marital problems or that she had a significant alcohol problem. Her husband, Ron, insists that her nights out were innocent and that she did not engage in any illicit activities.

The family continues to hold onto the belief that Sneha died helping others on 9/11. For them, this scenario provides a sense of peace compared to the alternative theories of foul play or voluntary disappearance.

The disappearance of Dr. Sneha Anne Philip remains an unsolved mystery, deeply intertwined with the tragic events of 9/11. Despite extensive investigations and numerous theories, no definitive answers have been found. Sneha's case highlights the complex interplay of personal challenges and extraordinary historical events, leaving her family and the public to grapple with unanswered questions.

Her story serves as a poignant reminder of the many lives irrevocably altered by the events of September 11, 2001, and the enduring quest for closure by those left behind.

Chapter Forty-One

Amy Fitzpatrick

AMY FITZPATRICK, a 15-year-old Irish girl, vanished on
New Year's Day in 2008 from Mijas Costa, near Málaga,

Spain. Her disappearance remains one of the most baffling mysteries of recent years, involving a combination of police investigations, eyewitness accounts, and multiple theories. This chapter provides a detailed account of the events surrounding her disappearance, the subsequent search efforts, and the theories that have emerged over time.

Amy Fitzpatrick moved to Spain in 2004 with her mother Audrey Fitzpatrick, her brother Dean, and her mother's partner, Dave Mahon. They settled in the tourist resort of Riviera del Sol on the Costa del Sol. On December 31, 2007, Amy spent the evening babysitting with her friend Ashley Rose at Ashley's house. She left around 10 PM on January 1, 2008, to walk the short distance back to her home, but she never arrived.

The initial search for Amy involved local police, volunteers, and her family. The search began almost immediately after she was reported missing. Despite extensive searches of the surrounding areas and coastlines, no trace of Amy was found. Early on, police speculated that Amy might have run away, but her family strongly believed otherwise, citing that she left behind her mobile phone and other personal belongings.

In August 2008, a significant lead emerged when the home of Amy's lawyer, Juan José de la Fuente Teixidó, was broken into. Stolen items included a laptop and Amy's Nokia mobile phone, both crucial to the investigation. The lawyer speculated that the burglary was related to Amy's disappearance, as the burglars left behind more valuable items and took documents related to the case.

In June 2009, Audrey Fitzpatrick received a disturbing phone call from a man claiming to know Amy's whereabouts. The caller demanded a ransom of €500,000, claiming that Amy had been kidnapped and was being held in Madrid. Despite the urgency, the call turned out to be a cruel hoax. The phone numbers used in the call were untraceable pre-paid numbers, and the lead went cold.

Over the years, various theories and suspects have emerged regarding Amy's disappearance:

1. Abduction by Strangers: The theory that Amy was abducted by someone she didn't know is supported by several unconfirmed sightings. Witnesses reported seeing a girl matching Amy's description with an older man in the hours following her last confirmed sighting.

2. Local Involvement: In 2012, rumors surfaced that Eric "Lucky" Wilson, an Irish gangland figure,

might have been involved in Amy's disappearance. Some believe that Amy was killed due to her association with older, more dangerous individuals. This theory gained traction when it was revealed that Amy had been seen with an older man, believed to be Wilson, on the night of her disappearance.

3. Human Trafficking: Another prevailing theory is that Amy was abducted and forced into human trafficking. The Costa del Sol has known issues with trafficking, and some of the unconfirmed sightings of Amy in the area lend credence to this possibility.

4. Murder: In May 2011, a police report indicated that three witnesses had come forward, claiming they saw Amy with a mystery blonde woman in the Trafalgar Bar in Calahonda hours after her last reported sighting. This information fueled the belief that Amy might have been murdered and that her body was disposed of to cover up the crime.

The investigation faced numerous challenges, including jurisdictional issues between Spanish authorities and Irish law enforcement. Audrey Fitzpatrick hired private investigators to assist in the search, including the same detectives who worked on the Madeleine McCann case. Despite these efforts, significant leads were few and far between.

The Fitzpatrick family endured additional heartbreak when Amy's brother, Dean, was fatally stabbed in 2013. Dave Mahon, Audrey's partner, was convicted of manslaughter in connection with Dean's death. This tragic event further complicated the already painful search for Amy, casting a shadow over the family.

In May 2023, a new witness came forward with information regarding Amy's disappearance. This witness claimed to have known Amy and provided details about individuals she was associating with before she disappeared. The witness suggested that Amy's disappearance was a direct consequence of these associations, pushing Spanish authorities to reconsider their initial assessments.

Amy Fitzpatrick's case remains open, with her family continuing to push for answers. In recent years, they have called for a cold case review at the European level, hoping to bring renewed attention to her disappearance. Despite the passage of time, the Fitzpatrick family remains determined to find out what happened to Amy and to seek justice.

The disappearance of Amy Fitzpatrick is a tragic mystery that highlights the complexities and heartbreak associated with missing persons cases. Despite extensive search efforts, numerous theories, and personal tragedies, Amy's fate remains unknown. The continued dedication of her family and investigators provides a glimmer of hope that one day, the truth will be uncovered.

* * *

CONTINUE WITH OTHER GREAT BOOKS BY ETHAN HAYES

About the Author

Ethan Hayes grew up in Oklahoma and moved to Texas when he attended Texas A&M. Upon graduation he was hired by Texas Parks and Wildlife and remained there until he retired twenty-two years later. He currently lives in southeast Texas with his wife and two dogs. When he's not spending time enjoying the outdoors and writing, he sips a cold beer on his front porch while listening to Bluegrass music.

* * *

Send in your encounter story:
encountersbigfoot@gmail.com

Also by Ethan Hayes

Also by Free Reign Publishing